'This book offers a h
of the Church's past l
the context of the
Written from a Meth
informed by the author's wide experience across the denominations, its challenging analysis will be found widely applicable.'
Margaret Jones, Methodist minister and historian.

'A prophetic wake-up call to British Methodism based on a clear, prayerful analysis of the problems we face. The hope-filled vision for the future lies in returning to prayerful repentance, the evangelical power of the Word of God, sacrificial service and, personal evangelism.'
Paul Wilson, Methodist minister, Development Worker, Methodist Evangelicals Together.

'Even when I disagree with him, Tom Stuckey has interesting things to say. This book offers many challenges to 21st century Christians located (as Tom argues) in a modern Babylonian captivity where we seek to tame God and fail to grasp that the cross exposes the darker side of human progress'.
Dudley Coates, Past Vice-President of the Methodist Conference.

'As ever Tom Stuckey brings a new perspective to our thinking about ecumenism and mission. Although written for Methodists what the author says about the Babylonian captivity of the Church in Britain is pertinent for Anglicans as well.'
> *Peter Hancock, Bishop of Bath and Wells.*

'Timely and real; a *cri de coeur* on the plight of today's Church gives us hope as we seek to survive and grow in our very own Babylonian exile.'
> *Bruce Thompson, Methodist minister, Chair of the Lincolnshire District.*

Singing the Lord's Song in a Strange Land

The Future of the Church in Britain: A Methodist Perspective

TOM STUCKEY

Copyright. Tom Stuckey 2019
All rights reserved

ISBN 9781073196647

Edition 2

DEDICATION

to
Michael Townsend and Angela Shier-Jones

who encouraged my faith in Methodism

and

Christine

who keeps my love and faith in God alive

Acknowledgements

I wish to thank the following who have contributed to the shaping and production of this book. John and Valerie Carne, David Coote, Margaret Jones, Gwyneth Owen, Neil Richardson, Christine Stuckey, Martin Turner, John Walker. I am especially indebted to the three members of our Theology Group, David, Margaret and John, who have unfailingly responded to my many last-minute requests for comments.

My thanks also to Bob Davies and the production team of CMPP who have rushed to get this book out for the 2017 Methodist Conference. As always my wife Christine has shown remarkable patience and understanding.

Through conversations, discussions and email messages, not only have the above people given me suggestions, critiques and corrections to the script but have encouraged me to keep going. I hold none of them responsible for what I have written

Contents

Acknowledgements
Preface

Part 1 VISION
1 The riches of his grace
2 The hope of your calling

Part 2 REALITY
3 Babylon
4 There and here
5 The Babylonian captivity of the Church
6 Methodism: Where are you?

Part 3 PROPHECY
7 Exile?
8 Methodism: Where will you be?
9 Wake up, Methodism!

APPENDIX
10   Dry bones

STUDY QUESTION

Books by Tom Stuckey

Preface

I laughed when someone at church said 'the Methodist Church is facing meltdown'. Meltdown implies overheating, fire, passion. There's not much of that in our local church unless you count the arguments we have over removing the pews. When I think about a church overheating I have this picture of 18th-century Methodists in Scunthorpe and Skegness falling down in ecstasy during worship and frothing at the mouth. Today if such overheating took place the minister in charge would halt the proceedings in the interest of health and safety.[1]

Something is very wrong with our church. Somehow we've managed to pour water on the burning bush and all we have left is wet ashes.[2] Has the Spirit abandoned us? Is the Church in Britain finished? I think not.

On 29th June 2004, I had a powerful dream. It occurred on the night before I knew of my nomination as Methodist President.[3] It was so vivid that it left me tossing and turning for the rest of the

Preface

night. Was it simply an anxiety dream or did it have prophetic significance?

> I was looking in terror across a ravaged landscape. In all directions I saw the littered remains of bodies, consumed, picked clean by birds, scattered by wild animals, scorched by the sun. A terrible battle had taken place. Now it was a desecrated graveyard. In the dream I had actually heard a voice repeating, 'Can these bones live? Can these bones live?'

This dream lay behind my Presidential Address, delivered in 2005 to our Representative Session of Conference meeting in Torquay.[4] Twelve years on, the question 'Can these bones live?' still haunts me. I am now retired. I continue to preach, teach, visit, give an occasional lecture, contribute to the *Methodist Recorder* and keep my own web site alive.[5] I have time to read, think, assess and pray.

Was my dream with its promise of Pentecost a delusion or was it really a prophetic vision? Did my Conference Address of 2005 (which I have included in the Appendix) fall on deaf ears? Was it all empty rhetoric? As churches continue to crumble I have come to see that Pentecost is about judgement as well as renewal. I spoke of repentance then. I speak of it now.[6]

The world situation has changed dramatically over the past ten years. The failure of the Arab spring, the advent of ISIS, the banking crisis, the

Preface

hubris of powerful elites, civil wars in Syria, the Yemen and Somalia, the flood of migrants, the ever growing gap between rich and poor, the rise of 'popularism' demonstrated in Brexit and the election of Donald Trump. On top of this the recent ravings coming from North Korea are ratcheting up levels of global volatility.

It has been suggested that the world is passing through a huge paradigm shift, the likes of which have not been seen for several generations.[7] According to Duncan Forester, writing in 2001, we no longer stand optimistically at the end of history but had entered a new age of terror where apocalyptic theology becomes an essential tool for the understanding and the stating of truth behind events.[8] This book is my response to Forester's challenge. The title gives the game away. The Church, I contend, exists in a Babylon which snaps, snarls and beguiles the people of God. I intend to describe this context, set out how it affects the Church before suggesting what the Church in Britain will look like in the future.

As a Methodist I realize that our church is a small player in the global mission of God. Churches rise and fall as Christians in a multiplicity of contexts respond or fail to respond to the promptings of the Holy Spirit. It should therefore be clear that I cannot comment on the future of Methodism without considering what is happening to the other churches in Britain. Furthermore,

Preface

church life here, as in Europe and America, has to be seen within the context of world Christianity. I have recently been reading some of Tony Benn's writings. He was a person who infuriated many. Some regarded him as a prophet. He did spend time in the wilderness before becoming a 'national treasure' in his old age. The old, he said, usually become pessimistic, but then adds that 'pessimism is a prison into which you incarcerate yourself'.[9] At the age of 85, Benn wrote of his surprise and delight in 'rediscovering idealism'. As I get older I too find myself becoming surprisingly optimistic. This optimism of hope does not spring from idealism. It springs from the Bible. Any particular part of the Bible? The letter to the Ephesians! As you read on you will find the Ephesian vision and hope transfiguring the message of this book.

About footnotes

Don't ignore them. Some are included to explain Methodist terms to the non-Methodist reader. Others are important glosses on the text. For Methodists worried about whether we shall still be here in twenty years time and who may be tempted to go immediately to the three chapters dealing with our church, I assure you that we do have a future though it will be very different from what you might expect. Dear readers, I encourage you to press on

Preface

chapter by chapter to discover what God might have in store for us all.

NOTES

1. I found this in an old church magazine. Source unknown.
2. John Pritchard, *Something More*, SPCK, 2016
3. The Conference is an annual gathering of representatives, ministerial and lay, of Methodists across Britain and from some of our sister Churches in other parts of the world. Each year they appoint a President who is to represent, and give leadership and inspiration, to the Church.
4. The Conference, meeting for about a week, travels to different locations in England. In its opening session the appointed President delivers an address of his or her choosing. It usually sets out the theme for the year.
5. Google: Tom Stuckey (home) www.tomstuckey.me.uk
6. 'In our talk of a God of love we have forgotten, that like the raging sea, God is dangerous. We have not only put God in a box but we have become so used to transporting God around in buckets that God has ceased to be God. We have tamed the terror. We have managed the mystery. One thing is required, "we must repent!"'. (Appendix 2:4)
7. Professor Martin Conway of Oxford has suggested that 2016 may well prove to be a liminal year of

Preface

significance like 1914 and 1945 when familiar ways of doing things came to an end.

8. Duncan Forester, *Apocalypse Now?* Ashgate Publishing Ltd, 2005, pp.50f.
9. Tony Benn, *The Last Diaries: A Blaze of Autumn Sunshine*, Ruth Winstone (ed.), Arrow Books, 2014.

Part 1

VISION

1

THE RICHES OF HIS GRACE

I pray that the God of our Lord Jesus Christ, the Father of glory, may give you a spirit of wisdom and revelation as you come to know him, so that, with the eyes of your heart enlightened, you may know what is the hope to which he has called you, what are the riches of his glorious inheritance amongst the saints, and what is the immeasurable greatness of his power to us who believe. (Eph. 1.17–19)

Paul had only ten years of active ministry and spent two of them in Ephesus. I have had nearly 50 years. My first appointment was a pastorate in Armadale, Scotland. Having to preach twice in the same church most Sundays forced me to hone my preaching skills. Fortunately I was also studying part-time at New College, Edinburgh, and this gave me the necessary theological equipment to feed the preaching.

My second appointment was on a council housing estate in Bristol where under the influence of the charismatic movement I discovered the experiential power of the Holy Spirit. Since then the context and scope of my ministry has widened, first in a city-centre church in Exeter with University Chaplaincy, then to inner city Manchester with a teaching post in the Northern Federation for Training in Ministry. The latter opened up opportunities to lecture overseas. Then I was sent to Reading as superintendent of a very large circuit with about 20 staff. The Reading circuit was my equivalent to Paul's Ephesus though the challenges were as nothing compared to difficulties Paul had to cope with.

Paul's circuit was huge. The six other churches apart from Smyrna were all were inland. To visit them you would have to journey hundreds of miles across the Western end of Asia Minor. It would take days. Ephesus, with its population of 250,000, was the provincial capital of Asia Minor and possibly the third largest city in the Empire after Rome and Alexandria.[1] The capital with its Empire was viewed by some as a re-incarnation of Babylon (1 Pet. 5.13). Paul, as a Roman citizen, appreciated many of its benefits and viewed it in a more kindly light. He was not however blind to the ungodliness, idolatry and wickedness (Rom. 1.18) found in its major cities. Strategically placed, Ephesus was a prosperous magical melting pot of religious cultures. Over fifty gods and goddesses were worshipped but Artemis reigned supreme. Her influence permeated the economics of the city.

Ephesus, probably more so than Rome, reflected an Asian culture in which people looked to the stars and shuddered. They felt that their lives were being determined by mysterious malign powers. To escape the tyranny of these unseen forces, they took to religion and superstition just as many today take to drink and drugs. Magic formulae and charms were like forged passports to an imaginary freedom. People escaped reality by embracing fantasy; again a growing feature of today. The 'principalities and powers' were cosmic forces rather than personal demons.[2] They impregnated the 'spiritual matrix' of Paul's world.

Every age has its own 'spiritual matrix'. Just as Ephesus had its Artemis, we in Britain have the omnipotent 'market god'. Artemis had her awesome temple. We have 'the City' and Canary Wharf. We should not delude ourselves into thinking that false gods disappear in an educated and scientific age like ours. They keep transmuting themselves to reappear in a new guise. Human beings keep creating false gods. These external spiritual powers have invaded our political and economic structures. They feed popularism and delusion. Their malign influence pollutes, distorts and corrupts.

Over and against these negativities, the letter to the Ephesians proclaims the wisdom, the wonder and the power of God. It holds up the vision of a world-wide transforming mission.[3] It presents us with the vision of a Trinitarian God of limitless resources who wants to shower immeasurable blessing upon us. 'I want you', says the writer, to have the power to comprehend with all the saints, what is the breadth and length and height and depth, and to know the love of Christ that surpasses knowledge, so that you may be filled with the fullness of God. (Eph. 3.14–19)

What sort of God?

The first chapter of Ephesians tells us that God is beyond the box. His presence even in Christ is beyond Christ as he floods the universe with Spirit (v.23). Any attempt to confine or define this God is like trying to catch the waves of the ocean in a fishing net. God is both everywhere and somewhere. This God is elusive and enigmatic. God can be present in his absence and even when he reveals himself he can assume a disguise. Moreover God is beyond gender.[4] It is all very confusing and mind-blowing; and so it should be if God is God.

The writer of Ephesians re-works the idea of monotheism (one God). You can see this happening in the first chapter as he tries to describe the relationship between God the Father and Jesus Christ. The phrase 'in him' and the pronoun 'he' is repeated several times. You have to keep asking yourself, does 'he' refer to the Father or to Jesus Christ? There appears to be a dynamic interactive relationship between them which is further complicated when the person of the Holy Spirit is introduced (v.13).[5] This interactive, community God ebbs and flows, mingles and moves to flood the universe with 'fullness' (1.23).

It is essential to grasp the idea of the fluidity of the Holy Spirit for our understanding of the mission of God. The Church's mission is to recognize where God is at work in the world and to join in. The problem is in discerning the Spirit's presence. It has been described in this way:

> God, who is everywhere, never leaves us. Yet he seems sometimes to be present, sometimes absent . . . He is like the wind that blows where it pleases. You who love him must love him as arriving from where you do not know and as going where you do not know.[6]

How does one describe this mysterious dynamic God who is Father, Son and Holy Spirit? You cannot put mystery on a dissecting table, though many have tried. The person of Job, in the Old Testament, after 40 chapters of arguing about suffering finally confesses, 'I have uttered what I do not understand, things too wonderful for me, which I did not know' (Job 42.3).

Using any label for God produces a false god. Should the word 'God' be discarded altogether? The slogan *There Is Probably No God* – which appeared on some London buses in 2009 – may not be as negative as some might suppose since the first Christians were called 'atheists' because they would not worship 'gods' like Artemis. God is not an 'object'. God is a 'subject' yet beyond subjects. 'God' should be regarded, grammatically, as a verb rather than as a noun.[7] Maybe the proper response is silence.

The first chapter of Ephesians is impregnated with worship words like 'blessed', 'praise', 'thanks', 'prayer' and 'faith'. Only through prayer can we begin to comprehend the mystery of God. This is why I have placed verses 17 to 19 at the head of this chapter. To understand you must 'stand under'.

Pentecostal break-ins

When in AD 53 Paul, having trekked across country, arrived at this bustling, cosmopolitan, sea-port city he immediately sought out the Christian congregation. Ten months before he had stopped off at Ephesus breaking his long sea journey from Corinth to Jerusalem. He left behind his two friends Priscilla and Aquila. They had planted a church. Members met in a number of homes but retained strong links with the synagogue. When an eloquent preacher called Apollos, an Alexandria Jew, arrived this church started to grow. Paul, on this visit, planned to stay longer since Apollos had gone off to minister in the Corinthian Church.[8] Would Paul be pleased with what the previous minister had done?

The Riches of His Grace

I imagine him looking around the synagogue at the congregation. His conclusion? 'You look half dead.' They had formality without vitality. The charismatic presence of the Holy Spirit was missing. Pentecost was unheard of. He preached about the Holy Spirit. Pentecostal power exploded. Ecclesiastical maintenance was transfigured into mission. You can read the story in Acts 19 though I have used a bit of poetic licence here.

If you scan through the Ephesian letter you will find references to the immeasurable 'riches of grace' (1.7, 2.7, 3.8, 3.16). The opening chapter lists them; redemption, forgiveness, knowledge of the divine purpose, a new inheritance and the seal of the Holy Spirit. In the initial Pentecostal transformation twelve people were personally affected. Paul, in chapter 2, contrasts the 'before' and the 'after'.

- Dead in transgressions BUT now alive in Christ.
- Imprisoned by the ruler of the air BUT now free in the heavenly realms of Christ.
- Driven by passions and desires BUT now saved by grace.
- Objects of wrath BUT now subjects of mercy.
- Outsiders without hope BUT now insiders with peace.
- Caught up in the ways of the world BUT now radiating kindness.

- Stumbling in the darkness BUT now walking in the light.
- Strangers and aliens BUT now members of God's household

Is he suggesting that the transformation is complete so that we leave the 'before' completely behind? Not so. Christians live in the overlap between the old and the new. We remain in this material three-dimensional world of earthly kingdoms, clocks, emails, Brexit and Donald Trump. We still have to get up, dress, have breakfast, and face the challenges of the day. This world of 'the before', according to Paul, is marked by distortion, greed, sin, depravity and delusion.

On the other hand, there is the unseen parallel universe of God's glorious 'after'. Its roots are in the future rather than the past. It is a world of light, anticipated in the resurrection of Christ. It exists alongside our world and occasionally breaks in to astonish, illuminate, energize and transform. Paul had personally experienced a divine 'break in'. On the Damascus Road the blinding light of the knowledge of the glory of God in the face of Jesus Christ shone into his heart. A 'break-in' happened at Pentecost in Jerusalem. A similar 'break-in' happened when Paul came to Ephesus, preached and laid hands on those nominal Christians so that 'they spoke in tongues and prophesied' (Acts 19.6). Because of the cross and resurrection the whole of our existence on earth is saturated with divine possibility. 'Break-ins' can happen at any time and in any place. Early Methodism records many divine 'breaks-ins'; some very gentle, others spectacular. John Wesley describes such an event on New Year's Day 1739.

> About three in the morning, as we were continuing instant in prayer, the power of God came mightily upon us, in as much that many cried out for exceeding joy, and many fell to the ground. As soon as we were recovered a little from that awe and amazement at the presence of His majesty we broke out with one voice, 'We praise Thee, O God; we acknowledge Thee to be the Lord.'[9]

A missionary movement

Paul wanted to go on using the Jewish synagogue as his base but hit opposition from some of the members. He therefore hires a secular hall next door, takes some of the members with him and plants a 'fresh expression' of Church. Now things really take off. After two years it is reported that the 'whole of Asia' heard the word of the Lord. Given the strategic, economic and geographical importance of the city and the network of Roman roads, Paul's message about the universal 'riches of grace' would have been taken to the outlying

The Riches of His Grace

regions by the thousands of travellers who flocked in and out of the city. Furthermore as Ephesus boasted one of the seven wonders of the ancient world, a temple devoted to the goddess Artemis, additional crowds of site-seers could be expected. Much of the civic wealth of Ephesus depended on religious tourism. The Christian message, because of its counter-cultural impact, could threaten the buoyant economy of the city. The Church's mission in fact so challenged the superstitions attached to the temple of Artemis that it provoked a riot amongst the sellers of religious knick-knacks. An explosion of grace can topple kingdoms. The early Methodists knew this as they sang:

> When he first the work begun,
> Small and feeble was his day:
> Now the word doth swiftly run,
> Now it wins its widening way;
> More and more it spreads and grows
> Ever mighty to prevail;
> Sin's strongholds it now o'erthrows,
> Shakes the trembling gates of hell.[10]

Embedded in the opening chapter of Ephesians are references to 'election', God's 'plan' (v.10) and God's 'choosing' (v.4). God's plan is to 'sum up' or summarize all things in Christ (v.10). This word suggests a 're-harmonization' of everything. Our world has become discordant; a cacophony of noise. It is more dissonant than the sounds an orchestra

The Riches of His Grace

makes when tuning up for a performance of a great symphony. I interpret what Paul is saying by using the analogy of an orchestral concert. Members of the orchestra (Christians) have been 'chosen' for a task. Christ, the conductor, steps onto the stage and enables the orchestra to create such inspired music that every member of the audience wants to become a performer. That's how 'election' works! As the Spirit inspires and moves in ever increasing waves across the world so the music of the Word moves from person to person drawing in more and more partners in mission. Methodism began as a missionary movement.

Wesley's focus was upon the Spirit of God burning like a fire in the hearts of converted individuals, renewing the Church, firing communities and spreading until scriptural holiness covers the whole earth. His vision was of the restoration and renewal of all things through grace.[11]

Ephesians presents a global vision of hope. We are chosen to be God's active agents in realizing the dream of a universe re-tuned to God's music. It is not God's repair job because the original plan had broken down; rather God the Trinity had this in mind from the beginning. 'He chose us in Christ' before the big bang of creation 'and predestined us in love, to be his own sons and daughters through Christ'. Our security in God is rooted beyond the stars of fate and the vagaries of economics and worldly powers.

The Riches of His Grace

The writer of the book of Revelation in his message of hope presents us with pictures of the rise and fall of Empires; Babylon toppled by Persia, Persia by Greece, Greece by Rome. Although Rome would become the new Babylon, she too would tumble. Christians would face opposition but there is no room for doom and gloom. Set-backs are mere blips along the way within the vast confines of time and space. God is re-harmonizing the whole of creation to the music of Christ who will flood all things with a fullness (v.22) which will transform and create a new heaven and a new earth. We have been invited as partners in mission to spread this good news of hope and salvation for all.

O that the world might taste and see
The riches of his grace!
The arms of love which compass me
Would all mankind embrace.[12]

NOTES

1. Was Alexandria or Antioch the second or third largest? There is lots of guesswork here.
2. 'Principalities and powers' occurs many times in the letters of Paul (Rom. 8.38; Eph. 1.21, 3.10, 6.12; Col 1.14, 2.10, 2.16; Titus 3.1). These 'powers' are similarly described by the reference to 'the prince of the power of the air' (Eph. 2.2).
3. Between 4th September 2008 and 6th August 2009, I wrote a series of twelve monthly articles for

the *Methodist Recorder* under the heading, 'Ephesians: An Answer to Credit Crunch'. In April 2009, at the first ever gathering of former Presidents and Vice-Presidents of the Methodist Church, I delivered a lecture entitled 'The Ephesian Moment'. Much of the material of these first two chapters has been drawn from those articles, the Presidential lecture and subsequent discussion.

4. Some people will refer to God as 'she'. For convenience sake only throughout this book I have referred to God as 'he'. God is beyond gender and yet at the same time both masculine and feminine. Some will assign gender roles to different persons of the Trinity. This is incorrect since it fails to recognize the nature of the shared life within the Trinity.

5. There is a sort of barn dance; a flow and flux going on within God; a finding and a losing, a circling and spiralling of partners until all three are transfigured in each other, lost in a love-making out of which new universes are conceived and born. When the Trinity turns towards the world, the Word and the Spirit become the two arms of God embracing all humanity. On the cross this dynamic partnership of Son, Spirit and Father is stretched to its ultimate limit to encompass and embrace the pain of the whole world. In the resurrection the partners hug each other and us in the joy of a world redeemed. So the Trinity, to change the imagery, is like a vast cosmic sea of

love ebbing and flowing; ever changing yet ever the same (Appendix 2:2).
6. José Comblin, *The Meaning of Mission*, Dublin: Gill & Macmillan, 1979, pp.44f.
7. Janet M. Soskice, *The Kindness of God: Metaphor: Gender and Religious Language*, Oxford University Press, 2007.
8. It is argued that the Apollos of Acts may not be the Apollos of Corinth. 1 Cor. 4.6 raises further doubts over my interpretation.
9. *The Journal of John Wesley*, Vol 2, N. Curnock (ed.), Epworth, 1938, p.121.
10. Hymn, H&P, 781.
11. Appendix 4:2.
12. Hymn, H&P, 264.

2

THE HOPE OF YOUR CALLING

Walk as children of light . . . Take no part in the unfruitful works of darkness but instead expose them . . . Awake, O sleeper, and rise from the dead and Christ shall give you light. Look carefully then how you walk, not as unwise men but as wise, making the most of the time, because the days are evil. Therefore do not be foolish but understand what the will of the Lord is. Do not get drunk with wine, for that is debauchery; but be filled with the Spirit. (Eph. 5.8–18)

1969 marked my first year in Scotland, and I preached thirty-nine sermons on Ephesians. I faced the same congregation every Sunday and Scottish Methodists were not keen on the lectionary. This letter has certainly entered my blood stream though it left the congregation somewhat exhausted from overkill. I have never again inflicted such an unrelenting repertoire on a congregation. Visiting Armadale in 2006 they still remembered the Ephesian ordeal.

The town of Reading was my 'Ephesian Moment' when, as Methodist Superintendent, I was able to realize a few of my dreams. I had hoped to stay until retirement but God had other things in store.

When Paul ceased to be Superintendent of the Ephesian circuit, his itinerant ministry took him back to Greece. He then set off for Jerusalem. On this sea-going voyage he receives a prophecy. It disturbs him so much that he breaks his journey and demands to see the Ephesian elders. 'Savage wolves from both within and without are going to savage the church not sparing the flock.' His words were greeted with shock and bewilderment (Acts 20.28). The occasion becomes more traumatic when he shares another 'word' he has been given. 'The Holy Spirit testifies to me in every city that imprisonment and persecutions are waiting for me in Jerusalem.' Luke, in a most poignant episode, describes the pain and outpouring of grief as the elders bid their final farewells. They will never see his face again. Their prayers at the quayside are mingled with tears.

Did Paul write this Ephesians? Most scholars agree that it was written some years after his execution.[1] Three clues encourage speculation. There are the references to 'I Paul a prisoner' (3.1, 4.1) and a couple of sentences at the end of the letter.

> So that you also may know how I am and what I am doing, Tychicus will tell you everything. He is a dear brother and a faithful minister in the

Lord. I am sending him to you for this very purpose, to let you know how we are, and to encourage your hearts. (6.21f)

I am assuming these to be the actual words of Paul and that Tychicus was with Paul in prison. He was then sent off to Ephesus to communicate Paul's vision of God's mission. Tychicus may also have carried Paul's letter to the Colossians. Paul, I suggest, did not write Ephesians rather Tychicus did. Maybe he wrote from notes, maybe from memory, maybe he was even quoting Paul.

A mission statement

Has your church produced a mission statement? In my travels I observe these fading mementos adorning notice boards. Church members usually struggle to remember what it says. The Ephesian mission statement is two-fold. The Church is 'to make all see God's hidden mysterious plan' (3.9), and 'to make God's wisdom known to the principalities and powers' (3.10). It is a mission of 'enlightening' and 'incarnating'.[2] The first strand addresses the Church. Through preaching and teaching, church members are told of God, his purpose for the world and of the immeasurable riches of grace available to them. The second strand is practical, social and political. Members are to *make known* this mystery to the 'rulers and authorities in heavenly places'. Here is incarnation and confrontation.

The Ephesian message for the Church throughout the ages is that God is flooding the cosmos with Spirit and liberating life; exposing the false gods who dominate our lives and breaking down barriers between nations, races and classes. Sadly, there is little evidence of this when we look about. Leonardo Boff, a Latin American theologian, wrote, 'a glance at history reveals the stubborn presence of an anti-history – a history of evil, suffering, violence, and crime of immense dimensions.'[3] Is this Ephesian vision unattainable? Paul the realist takes the long view. His letter in acknowledging both 'mystery' and the presence of the 'principalities and powers' recognizes the ebb and flow of good and evil within nations and civilizations. He also gives us a picture of the Church expanding and contracting; disappearing in one place only to reappear in another as the Holy Spirit renews and judges. The tidal flow of the Spirit across the globe demonstrates the strength and the fragility of the Church and the difficulty of establishing justice.

Astronauts floating above the earth in outer space observing our blue planet have commented on the absence of artificial borders separating peoples and nations. That is the big picture – the Ephesian picture – a world without walls. The writer attempts to motivate his readers by reminding them that they were all outsiders once. He probably had in mind the dividing wall in the Jerusalem temple with its inscription 'No foreigner is to enter within the forecourt and the balustrade around the sanctuary.' He also knew that every physical barrier is supported by an ideology of exclusion. Paul believed that Christ's death had destroyed the walls of partition. Hospitality is to replace hostility.

Our world is full of walls. As soon as one barrier falls another is erected. Racism, xenophobia, religious tribalism and fear keep the wall building business going. When the Ephesian letter was written the Jerusalem temple lay in ruins; its city walls heaps of rubble. Tragically today a new wall has appeared there. Paul believes all walls can be toppled by the trumpet blast of the Gospel. A world without walls resembles an *'oikos'*; the Greek word for 'house'. *'Oikos'* is the root word for 'ecumenical', 'ecology' and 'economics'. Paul and Silas were accused of turning 'the *oikoumene* upside down' (Acts 17.6). On their anti-wall mission they hit opposition wherever they went. People cling to their protective barriers. Demolition work is dangerous.

Christian believers are urged to confront the powers of darkness and shine as beacons of light (5.11). The conflict between light and darkness reaches a climax in 6.10f. The Roman legionary becomes Paul's inspiration. Soldiers require body armour to protect themselves. As foot-soldiers seeking to secure a victory for justice and peace we too must carry defensive equipment; the helmet of salvation, the shield of faith, the belt of truth, the breastplate of righteousness and the sandals of peace. Our only weapon is the sword of the Spirit (6.16–17). Above all we must stand firm. Charles Wesley catches the spirit of Ephesians in his militant hymn.

> Soldiers of Christ arise
> And put your armour on,
> Strong in the strength which God supplies
> Through his eternal Son;
> From strength to strength go on,
> Wrestle and fight and pray,
> Tread all the powers of darkness down,
> And win the well-fought day.[4]

The removal of the dividing ideological wall between Jew and Gentile was the first wave of a series of Spirit movements which would sweep through the centuries battering on the fences of exclusion. Not all fences however can be destroyed but they can be moved.[5] Christians are called to be fence movers. Ultimately all walls will be destroyed as the Spirit replaces them with wells.[6]

A church fit for purpose

If we are to remove the walls of division and confront the oppressive powers which hide within institutions and governments then besides defensive armour we need powerful artillery. The writer describes how the resurrection has triggered an unprecedented showering of gifts. These grace gifts (*charismata*), given to the Church, are the 'power tools' of mission.

In 4.8 the writer quotes Psalm 68.18. The psalmist employs the analogy of a triumphant general returning home from the wars. He heads a procession of vanquished kings and captured booty. The rejoicing citizens, in their exuberance, shower gifts of flowers and adulation upon their conquering hero. The writer of Ephesians however deliberately changes the last part of the analogy. The original 'receiving' of gifts now becomes the 'giving' of gifts which are subsequently listed. These gifts are linked with the specific ministries of apostle, prophet, evangelist, pastor and teacher. These are bequeathed to the Church so that the body of Christ can be built up 'until all of us come to the unity of the faith and of the knowledge of the Son of God, to maturity, to the measure of the fullness of Christ' (4.13).

As I sat in worship the other Sunday the person leading the intercessions prayed that we might have a 'full church' and added 'I'm sure we all want this!' Whether the addition was meant for us or for God I am not sure. Although Ephesians speaks of 'fullness' I suspect that the writer of the letter would have been uncomfortable with what the worship leader was saying though he would certainly want the Church to grow. Orlando Costas, a theologian from South America lists four dimensions of growth: *numerical*, *conceptual*, *organic* and *incarnational*.[7]

The Ephesian Christians are not to be like 'infants, tossed back and forth by the waves and blown here and there by every wind of teaching' (4.14). They are rebuked for their spiritual and intellectual malnutrition. They are stuck in the 'adolescent phase' of Christian development. They lack *conceptual* growth. A growing Church is not a managed organization like the NHS but a symbiotic organism 'joined and held together by every supporting ligament' and building 'itself up in love as each part does its work' (Eph. 4.16). Church structures must always be flexible and fluid. Churches must never be micromanaged. This is what Costas means by *organic* growth.

Lastly *incarnational* growth relates to the degree to which the Church participates in the afflictions of the world and confronts injustice. This is the acid test. If a church is not engaged in liberating action on behalf of the weak, the destitute and the powerless then in spite of whatever else might be going on, it has lost its integrity.

The writer, in the rest of chapter 4, blasts away at immorality and unseemly conduct. He is telling us that if the Church is to grow it must rid itself of the 'futile thinking' (v.17). He is referring to those external cultural values which have been absorbed into the church and distort its life.

The ongoing struggle

On 24th August 1744, John Wesley preached in Oxford on the text 'They were all filled with the Holy Spirit'. William Blackstone sat in the congregation and afterward wrote:

> We were last Friday entertained at St Mary's by a curious sermon from Wesley the Methodist. He informed us first that there was not one Christian among all the heads of houses . . . that pride, avarice, luxury and drunkenness were general characteristics of the Fellows and that the students were a generation of triflers'. Blackstone was clearly upset and so too was the Vice Chancellor because of the resentment it had stirred up.[8]

Wesley, like the writer of Ephesians, was putting the bugle to his lips and blasting out a reveille call: 'Wake up' (5.14) and 'understand what the Lord's will is' (5.17). The instruction follows 'be filled with the Spirit' (5.18). The Greek verb is in the imperative mood and this makes it an obligatory command. It is in the plural form; all are to be filled as on the Day of Pentecost. In Greek there are two kinds of imperative, the 'aorist' and the 'present'. The 'aorist' tense describes a single completed action. Here the instruction is in the 'present' tense which in effect tells us to 'keep on being filled with the Spirit'. Why? Because we are leaky! We have to be filled every day. Finally the verb is passive. We do not fill ourselves, rather we allow the Holy Spirit to fill us – but here is the rub; God will only fill us when we have emptied ourselves. He takes the responsibility for the filling; we through repentance have the responsibility for the emptying.

The structure of Ephesians can be organized under three commands, 'sit', 'walk' and 'stand'. It captures the 'get up and go' of the writer. We 'sit' in chapters 1 and 2 to contemplate all that God has done until we are bathed in blessings and energized by praise. In chapters 3, 4 and 5, we are encouraged by the example of Paul to 'walk' (4.1, 17; 5.2, 8, 15 – most translate 'walk' as 'live'). The word 'stand' in chapter 6 is doubly underlined (verses 11 and 14). It can come as a shock to discover that this letter, which opens with a triumphant celebration of worship, ends with a declaration of war. This is because the overarching principalities and powers keep ignoring the news that they are defeated (3.10) and blindly attempt last-ditch retaliations with all the forces at their disposal. As mentioned in Chapter 1, we live in the overlap of two ages. The 'powers' will not be totally vanquished until the consummation.[9] The

Ephesian Church is being warned that it has an epic struggle on its hands if it is to survive and thrive.

The final verses are a call to prayer (6.18–20). The Ephesian letter is parceled up in prayer. Prayer begins in chapter 1 with the petition that 'we might see and know the riches of his grace'. It ends with the injunction to 'pray in the Spirit at all times' (6.18) and be specific in our prayers. The Ephesian vision reminds us of the hope of our calling. Methodism was inspired by this vision.

> Shine on thy work, disperse the gloom,
> Light in thy light I then shall see;
> Say to my soul: 'Thy light is come,
> Glory divine is risen on thee,
> Thy warfare's past, thy mourning's o'er;
> Look up, for thou shalt weep no more![10]

The Methodist scholar Gordon Rupp likened the Church to Cinderella, a figure, dirty and maligned, yet he insisted that she would get to the ball to be the bride of Christ.[11] The striking of the midnight clock announces a great reversal in which the ugly sisters of oppression are finally confounded. Ephesians (3.10) insists that the Church's very vulnerability pronounces death upon the rowdy powers who are always trying to drown out the quiet voice of God. Let Andrew Lincoln have the last word:

> What now becomes clear is that the Church

provides hostile cosmic powers with a tangible reminder that their authority has been decisively broken and that all things are subject to Christ. The overcoming of barriers between Jews and Gentiles, as they are united through Christ in the church, is a pledge of the overcoming of all division when the universe will be restored to harmony in Christ.[12]

NOTES

1. I am heavily dependent on Andrew Lincoln's, *Ephesians: Word Biblical Commentary* (Nash-ville: Nelson, 1990) for my exposition of this letter. I have, however, engaged in a lot of imaginative speculation in this section and not all New Testament scholars would support my theory.
2. Lincoln, pp.184f.
3. Leonardo Boff, *Passion of Christ, Passion of the World: The Facts, Their Interpretation, and Their Meaning Yesterday and Today*, New York, Orbis Books, 1987.
4. Hymn, H&P, 719.
5. Donald Messer in his book, *A Conspiracy of Goodness* (Nashville: Abingdon Press, 1992), describes the Church as a 'community of fence movers' (pp.128–144).
6. Tom Stuckey, *Beyond the Box*, Inspire, 2005, pp.20f.
7. Orlando Costas, *The Church and its Mission: A Shattering Critique from the Third World*, Wheaton:

8. Sermon IV 'Scriptural Christianity', *Wesley's Standard Sermons Vol 1*, E. H. Sugden (ed.), Epworth, 1966, pp.87f.
9. Lincoln, p.186.
10. Hymn, H&P, 529.
11. Gordon Rupp, *The Old Reformation and the New*, London: Epworth. 1967, p.62.
12. Lincoln, p.194.

Part 2
REALITY

3

BABYLON

Cargoes of gold, silver, jewels and pearls, fine linen, purples silk and scarlet, all kind of scented wood, all articles of ivory, all articles of costly wood, bronze, iron and marble, cinnamon, spices, incense, myrrh, frankincense, wine, olive oil, choice flour and wheat, cattle and sheep, horses and chariots, slaves, human bodies and souls. (Rev 17.12–13)

The body of Christ is the saving creation of God the Trinity. The city of Babylon is the supreme creation of the principalities and powers. The vision of the former dominates the opening chapters of Ephesians. The principalities and powers snarl at us at the end the letter. This chapter describes aspects of the Babylonian vision, its dominating policies, strategies and existence. The glory of Babylon is built on money, power, and control. Hubris and oppression are the outcomes.

The Biblical text heading this chapter is an inventory of the goods and traffic which once flowed in and out of the ancient city of Babylon. This monolith was known for its oppressive cruelty and materialism. Under Nebuchadnezzar (605–562 BC), Babylon undertook a series of aggressive military excursions conquering and subduing all who stood

Babylon

in its path. Babylon maintained dictatorial control by genocide, the deportation of the leadership classes and the relocation of whole populations.[1] The totalitarianism of the Babylonian State demands an acceptance of its values and material gods. Its massive ziggurats were symbols of glory and oppression.

We in Britain once conquered nearly half the globe. The patriotism which created the British Empire is now gone. Today we serve the god of consumerism and worship him in our cathedral-like shopping malls. Babylon had its ziggurats. In London we demonstrate our delight in the money god in the profusion of the towering of skyscrapers monstrously designed to shock and awe. Many are built with Russian, Arab and Chinese money. Their plush apartments stand empty most of the time while London's teachers, nurses, police officers and refuse collectors are forced to commute 20 or 30 miles each day.

Babylon is both a city and a Whore, a term used to signify luxury, sensuality, sexuality, seduction and allure. Although her appearance in the book of Revelation is magnificent (Rev 17), she is not to be trusted for she rides upon a beast of corruption. She is a celebrity who loves to be looked at yet takes even greater delight in gazing at herself.[2] She is the mythological origin of the 'selfie'. The message of Revelation is clear. Beware lest you are beguiled by her charms and drawn into the emptiness which she personifies. There is irony in her end. She is devoured in a most violent way by the beast on which she rides (17.16). Babylon is a culture of oppression and seduction. It will first swallow others before wreaking havoc upon its own people.

Babylon sponsors violence and war

Walter Brueggemann, writing in 2010, suggested that Christians within the US are living in a contemporary Babylon. The United States he says is shamelessly aggressive. It has a 'predator economy that seizes resources, imposes a certain culture, does immense damage to the environment, and leaves many societies in poor shape by a pattern of intrusion and departure.'[3]

Martin Bell, a onetime independent MP, suggests that violence has become an acceptable part of British culture.[4] It is being enacted in obvious things like pornography, video games, drug abuse, slave trafficking, rape, theft, and pillage. Harming others has also become common-place in families, organizations and businesses. Stanley Hauerwas, as far back as 1999, wrote:

> The ultimate pathos of our times is that we live in societies and polities formed by the assumption that there is literally nothing for which it is worth dying. The irony is that such

Babylon

societies cannot live without war as they seek to hide in war the essential emptiness of their commitments.[5]

The Babylonian Empire was created by war and maintained through violent oppression. Modern Babylons now have technological weapons millions of times more deadly. Sophisticated drones, the use of poisonous gas and hastily constructed barrel bombs fall indiscriminately from the skies to maim and destroy. The civil wars in Syria, Somalia and elsewhere have led to vast movements of people who flee the destruction of their homelands. The stream of migrants into Europe has become an unstoppable flood. In Britain we fear lest some of those who return from bloody conflicts might wish to wreak their own personal vengeance on our Western way of life which they believe to be destroying all they hold dear. Terry Waite suggests that we have unconsciously slipped into a third world war.[6]

The enemy amongst us has no distinguishing marks. We cannot tell friend from foe. We look with suspicion at the stranger with a beard carrying a large haversack. Being friendly and hospitable has become more risky. The Ephesian vision is of a world with walls removed. Many, in our 'free world' want to build walls to keep the stranger out.

Justin Welby in his Christmas sermon spoke of the economics of despair and how our world has 'become awash with fear and division.' The nuclear ambitions and provocative rhetoric of Kim Jong-un ratchets up the tension. Many fear that the unpredictability and inexperience of President Trump will launch us fully into World War III.

Ephesians ends with a call to arms but it is a different fight with different weapons. Paul's word to them and to us is clear.

> You must no longer live as the Gentiles live, in the futility of their minds. They are darkened in their understanding, alienated from the life of God because of their ignorance and hardness of heart. They have lost all sensitivity and have abandoned themselves to licentiousness, greedy to practice every kind of impurity. That is not the way you learnt Christ! (4.17–19)

The life-style of Babylon is destroying the planet

The Great Whore holds a golden cup full of abominations (Rev. 17.4) she climaxes the seven last plagues and ecological disasters. Plague, disease, famine, food shortages and death are natural consequences of the Babylonian war machine. The book of Revelation was written at a time when such calamities were occurring.[7] These were interpreted as signs of God wrath. Now we see them in the main as a consequence or our allegiance to Babylon's seductions.

Tons of plastic are being dumped into the sea to poison the oceans and choke marine life. Animals, birds, and valuable plants are being wiped out through poaching, illegal logging and the trafficking of rare species. Money and quick profits are driving these abominations. Toxic air pollution in London and elsewhere has hit record levels. A study of 146 monitoring stations recorded nitrogen dioxide levels breaching the World Health Organization guidelines, yet we are still seduced by our diesel vehicles.

There is a rabbinic comment that when God finished creating he showed Adam all the glories of nature. 'Behold the beauty of this world', he said. 'I am handing it over to you. Be careful that you do not damage it, for if you do, there will be no one left to mend it.'

The Hebrews believed the earth stood on two pillars: a pillar of justice and a pillar of righteousness (Ps. 97.2).[8] If a crack appeared in either due to human violation, the ecological system would become unbalanced (Ps. 82). If a serious rupture occurred, then the primal chaotic waters, which in Hebrew mythology were held back by the dome of the heavens and fabric of the earth, would pour in to destroy all life. This is what happened in the Old Testament flood.

There is a symbiotic relationship between ourselves, the plants, the animals, the air and the earth. We not only live in the planet, the planet lives in us. In his popular book *The Revenge of Gaia* James Lovelock dares to suggest that if we fail to take care of the earth, the earth will surely take care of itself by making us no longer welcome.[9]

In 2015, for the first time in history, carbon dioxide levels in our atmosphere reached the 'symbolic threshold' as emissions rate increased yet again. The world is in a new era of 'climate change reality'. We do not need the four horsemen of the apocalypse (Rev. 6) to destroy us. We are galloping to our own annihilation. Isaiah anticipates this grim scenario.

> The earth shall be utterly laid waste and utterly despoiled;
> for the Lord has spoken this word.
> The earth dries up and withers . . .
> The earth lies polluted under its inhabitants;
> for they have transgressed laws,
>   violated statutes, broken the everlasting covenant.
> Therefore a curse devours the earth and its inhabitants suffer for their guilt. (Isaiah 14.3f)

We live in an individualistic culture of self assertiveness

A Babylonian culture oppresses and seduces. Timothy Keller describes two types of culture: the culture of 'self-sacrifice' and the culture of 'self-assertion'.[10] Most in our Western Babylon live by a narrative of 'self-assertion'. My worth and identity depends on the dignity I bestow on myself. It is perfectly proper to detach oneself from ones community and abandon the values once held. Seduced by the allure of the Whore of Babylon my philosophy becomes 'I am at the centre of my world and I can do my own thing'. Do we not realize that this can end in emptiness? This philosophy is popularized in the song Elsa sings in the Walt Disney movie *Frozen*.

> It's time to see what I can do
> To test the limits and break through
> No right, no wrong, no rules for me.
> I'm free! [11]

The narrative of 'self sacrifice' is to be found in tribal and pre-modern cultures. The Kenyan born theologian John Mbiti describes it in this way:

> Only in terms of other people does the individual become conscious of his own being, his duties, his privileges and responsibilities towards himself and towards other people . . . The individual can only say, 'I am because we are; and since we are, therefore I am.'[12]

Like Adam and Eve in the garden we believe we can be 'like God'. The traditional Hebraic and Christian God has been replaced by the money God. John Hull encourages us to 'blaspheme the money God'.[13] Through the processes of globalization the money market does generate prosperity yet is blind to justice and creates wealth for the few who have and poverty for those who have not.

Alan Bennett describes Britain as having an ideology masquerading as pragmatism but where 'profit is the sole yardstick against which all our institutions must be measured, a policy which comes from . . . false assumptions about human nature, with greed and self-interest taken to be its only reliable attributes'.[14]

In 2009 we heard about the dark secrets of MPs' expenses. Initially those with questionable claims hid behind the rules, unwilling to admit they had done anything wrong.[15] Some months before there had been a public outcry against the extravagant bonuses awarded to certain top bankers whose recklessness had plunged the nation into debt. People were asking how Sir Fred Goodwin could walk away with a £16.9 million pay off. Next was Peter Cummings the former head of corporate banking at HBOS. Now it is Sir Philip Green, who sold off the British Home Stores and left his employees with a depleted pension pot. Do people of wealth and power have no shame? Sir Philip has attempted some form of redress. What has prompted this?

These examples illustrate how the Western narrative of 'self-assertion' can in Babylon generate such hubris that when things go wrong personal accountability is denied. Actions like these undermine institutions, create distrust, feed anger and widen the gap between those with power and those without it. Is the rise of 'popularism' a protest movement of the grass roots over and against our political masters and a nameless wealthy elite who control our lives?

Alasdair MacIntyre, in 1981, predicted that we in the Western World would enter a new Dark Ages. His prophetic comment has come true, 'The barbarians are not waiting beyond the frontiers; they have already been governing us for some time.'[16]

On 6th August 2011, we were given another example of the 'self-assertive' narrative; this time from the 'bottom' rather than the 'top'. An outbreak of rioting, looting, and burning started in Tottenham and spread across London. The skyline was tinged with smoke as London burnt. Similar outbreaks of violence occurred in Liverpool, Birmingham, Bristol and Manchester. By the twelfth of August 1,486 arrests had been made. It was not only teenage gangs who had gone on the looting spree but teenagers from the suburbs. Jonathan Sacks comments:

> What we have witnessed is a real, deep seated and frightening failure of morality. They were not rebels with or without a cause. They were mostly bored teenagers, setting fire to cars for fun and

looting shops for clothes, shoes, electronic gadgets and flat-screen televisions. If that is not an indictment of the consumer society, what is? . . . Civilization just caught a glimpse of its soul. We have just seen ours and it is not pleasant.[17]

Andrew Marr, at the end of his six hundred page *History of Modern Britain*, concludes, 'this history has told the story of the defeat of politics by shopping' aided by the 'great car economy'.[18] Vince Cable, in his analysis of Britain's 'credit-crunch', argues that anyone with a grasp of history will know that greed and stupidity are recurrent features in every civilization. Credit-crunch happened because honour within the banking industry had disappeared and the regulations of law were ineffective. Cable says, 'the amoral, cynical financial dealings which, we were assured, created wealth have not only contributed to instability but to a weakening of the wider social contract'. Presumption has ended in retribution, or in Cable's words: 'hubris is giving way to nemesis'.[19]

The fall of Babylon?

Many in the West rejoice at the passing of religion yet the current fantasy that secularism can replace religion has led to a return of religion in its most belligerent form. We have built new temples to a material god like the inhabitants of Paul's Ephesus and worship the idols of self. Babylon is a culture of oppression and seduction. Its philosophy is 'God is money, happiness is consumption and image is all'. The soul of Babylon is emptiness. This nihilism can, for a few individuals, acquire such potency that their hatred of the system and of themselves drives them to suicide. Babylon provides the soil for the production of the suicide bomber. ISIS provides an ideology to give credence for a crusade of death. Is it surprising that many teenagers are anxious and bored, that increasing numbers of people feel unsafe or that others want to put up the barricades.

There are three huge references to Babylon in Scripture (Isaiah 13, 14; Rev. 18). They all describe her sudden demise. In one hour she is laid waste and her life extinguished. Is there a suggestion here that Babylon's foundations have been undermined by the blood of the prophets and the saints (Rev. 18.24)?

Brueggemann in his observation of what was happening in the US in 1999 spoke of a huge paradigm shift taking place.

> It is abundantly and unmistakably clear that we are in a deep dislocation in our society that touches every aspect of our lives. It is a deep displacement and perhaps a transition, though none of us can yet see the completion of the transition.[20]

Professor Martin Conway of Oxford has suggested that 2016 may well prove to be a liminal year of significance like 1914 and 1945 when familiar ways of doing things came to an end.[21]

A twittering Trump is but a symptom of our entry into an ostrich age of denial where increasing numbers of people hide within fantasies of their own creating. Has truth become anything you want it to be? Not according to Ephesians (1.13, 4.21, 4.25, 5.9).

Stand therefore and fasten the belt of truth around your waist and put on the breastplate of righteousness. (6.14)

NOTES

1. Walter Brueggemann, *Out of Babylon*, Nashville: Abingdon Press, 2010, pp.13f.
2. N. and A. O'Hear, *Picturing the Apocalypse*, Oxford, 2015, pp.156f.
3. Brueggemann, p.127.
4. Martin Bell, *Through Gates of Fire: A Journey into World Disorder*. London: Weidenfeld and Nicolson, 2003, pp.1–3.
5. Stanley Hauerwas, *After Christendom*, Nash-ville: Abingdon Press, 1991, p.44.
6. Terry Waite, *Taken on Trust: 25th Anniversary Edition*, 2016 (Kindle).
7. In AD 65 a terrible plague visited Rome. There were

chronic earthquakes in Asia Minor and the towns of Laodicea and Colossae were laid waste in AD 60. Vesuvius erupted in AD 79.
8. Matthew Fox, *Original Blessing*, New Mexico: Bear & Co, 1983, p.184.
9. James Lovelock, *The Revenge of Gaia*, Allen Lane, 2006.
10. Timothy Keller, *Making Sense of God: An Invitation to the Sceptical*, H&S, 2016, p.120
11. Keller, p.121.
12. Hulley, Kretzschmar and Pato (eds.), *Arch-bishop Tutu: Prophetic Witness in South Africa*, Cape Town: Human and Rousseau, 1996, p.137.
13. John Hull's suggestions found in Chris Rowland and John Vincent, *British Liberation Theology 6: Radical Christianity, Roots and Fruits*, UTU, 2016, pp.9f
14. Alan Bennett, *Keeping On, Keeping On*, London: Faber, 2016.
15. The sleaze continues. At the time of writing (April 2017) 24 Conservative MPs are being investigated for criminal offences in regard to their election expenses.
16. Alasdair MacIntyre, *After Virtue: A Study in Moral Theory*, London: Duckworth, 1981, p.245.
17. Jonathan Sacks, *Celebrating Life: Finding Happiness in Unexpected Places*, London: Continuum, 2004, p.48.
18. Andrew Marr, *History of Modern Britain*, London:

Macmillan, 2007, p.597. Not all will agree with Marr's conclusion.
19. Vince Cable, *The Storm: The World Economic Crisis and What it Means*, London: Atlantic Books, 2009, p.52,
20. Walter Brueggemann, *Deep Memory Exuberant Hope: Contested Truth in a Post-Christian World*, Fortress Press, 2000, p.59.
21. An article in the '*I*' newspaper on 30th December 2016.

4

THERE AND HERE

Where is the one who brought them up out of the sea with the shepherds of his flock? Where is the one who put within them his Holy Spirit? (Isaiah 63.11)

Ephesians begins with the vision of a Trinitarian God filling the cosmos with vitality and light. This is not a description of our contemporary world! Foul pollution, over consumption, depleted resources, unprecedented levels of debt, fear, uncertainty, destabilizing hedonism; these are the grim realities of Babylon! God seems to have taken a back seat leaving the principalities and powers in charge. The Church in Britain inhabits the struggling end of Ephesians not its exuberant beginning. It is a depressing picture yet it is only half the story. Every day fifty thousand people become Christians.[1] If we ask with Isaiah 'where is the one who brought us up out of the sea?' the answer is clear. Deliverance and regeneration is taking place 'there' rather than 'here'. The Church is growing amongst people who inhabit a culture of 'self-sacrifice' rather than our culture of 'self-assertion'.

There and Here

Christians 'there' – The Church beyond Europe and North America

In 1893, 80% of the Christians in the world lived in Europe and North America. Now almost 60% of Christians throughout the world live in Africa, Asia, Latin America and the Pacific. In 1900 there were 10 million African Christians; now there are 400 million, the larger percentage of these being found in the African indigenous churches. Last Sunday in each of the nations of Nigeria, Kenya, Uganda, Tanzania and South Africa there were more Anglicans in church than in the whole of Britain and the United States combined.[2]

In China during the 1980s Christianity grew rapidly in the countryside stimulated by the collapse of local health care. The Christian contagion has now spread to the cities. Growth has been so rapid that there are now more Christians in China than members of the Communist Party (87 million). In Latin America, once the bastion of Roman Catholicism, Pentecostalism has transformed the Christian landscape. It has been estimated that by 2050 only about one fifth of the world's three billion Christians will be non-Hispanic whites. The era of Western Christianity has passed away within my lifetime.[3]

There and Here

Because of our previous 'sending' role we continue to assume that the West is still the centre of the Christian world thus giving us the right to set the agenda. When Paul began his work in the synagogue of Ephesus growth was confined. It was only when he moved to a different location where old traditions no longer prevailed that Word and Spirit came together in power. We are still the 'Mother Church' but we have become arthritic. The future of Christianity lies beyond our shores.

Why is the Spirit so potent there rather than here? There are many reasons. For a start, most of the growth is taking place among the poor.[4] Second, their churches are nearly all lay-led. Third, the churches affirm the traditional Biblical faith and make real demands upon their members. Fourth, they use the music, symbols and oral traditions of their local communities. Fifth, they believe in prayer and in the power of the supernatural.

Unlike our culture of 'self-assertion' theirs is made up of extended families who inhabit a narrative of 'self-sacrifice'.[5] Here individuals have to be converted one at a time. There people become Christian through corporate groups and extended families. Even when those from the rural areas migrate to cities and detach themselves from their traditional communities, the self-sacrifice narrative lingers. Moreover the transitional experience of anomie (rootless-ness) makes migrants receptive to

There and Here

any expression of faith which offers identity and a new sense of belonging. These factors help the growth of Islam as well as Christianity.

This is not to say that the 'Christians there' have got the answer. Many of the churches reflect the patriarchal cultures in which they flourish. There is a homophobic and sexist shadow side which they are not always willing to confront. The seeking of personal power and status by men within the church also has a corroding influence.

Christians 'here' – The Church in Britain, Europe and North America

John V. Taylor, one-time bishop of Winchester, puts his finger on our problem.

> I have not heard recently of a committee meeting adjourned because those present were still awaiting the arrival of the Spirit of God. I have known projects abandoned for lack of funds, but not for lack of the gifts of the Spirit. Provided the human resources are adequate we foolishly take the spiritual for granted.[6]

While this is undoubtedly true, our consumer context and our culture of 'self-assertion' has compounded our difficulties.

Callum Brown in his scholarly book, *The Death of Christian Britain*, charts the relentless decline of our churches and pours scorn on the facile

There and Here

responses of church leaders who naively think they can reverse the process by changing the structure of their organization or their liturgy. He argues that the problem goes far back to the 1800s. Up to then Christian piety had been primarily located in masculinity but then gradually moved to femininity. In the last century the nature of femininity changed radically, shed its veneer of personal piety and in the 1960s disappeared altogether as women sought fulfilment outside of the church.[7] He concludes that the Church in Britain will continue to exist but in a skeletal form with an increasing commitment from decreasing numbers. 'Britain is showing the world how religion as we have known it can die.'[8]

The explosion in the 1990s of new leisure-time opportunities at weekends further hastened the decline of church going. From 1995 the culture of Babylon really started to bite. Instead of going to church, ten times as many people were making their offering to God by driving to out-of-town shopping malls. In addition Center Parks provided an exciting place for families to spend quality time together as an alternative to church or dialling-up the internet.

Michael Riddell concludes that the Church in Britain has become the greatest barrier to the Gospel.[9] Locked in an iron cage and controlled by an ecclesiastical elite of clergy and powerful lay persons, it has become a stagnant pool.[10]

Inherited church and emerging church.

While the Roman Catholics have the one primary model of 'inherited church', the rest of us have embraced the more recent model of 'emerging church'. This operates alongside the traditional one. 'Inherited church' has been defined by the formula:[11]

church = building + priest + stipend

Cathedrals are the 'flagships' of 'inherited church'. Most 'inherited churches' lack the historical appeal of a cathedral. They generally have or share a minister or priest and are more reliant on a small band of unpaid volunteers many of whom have grown up in that church. These loyal volunteers are committed 'to keeping their church going'.

New 'emerging churches' do not always employ a minister/leader nor necessarily have a building of their own. They too are dependent on a small group of leaders. The leadership team is usually made up of visionary, committed, praying and believing volunteers. Their message is evangelical and more reliant on the Holy Spirit. They make discipleship demands on those who attend. 'Emerging church' unlike 'inherited church' with their buildings and ministerial systems, has the flexibility to move quickly and tailor their 'liturgical product' to the specific and ever changing needs of younger people, mobile families and groups.

Inherited church	Emerging church
members	*disciples*
solid	*liquid*
faithful	*full of faith and the Holy Spirit*
keep the church going	*increase numbers attending*
liturgy rooted in the past	*liturgy shaped for the present*
structure and systems mostly fixed	*structure and systems fluid*

What now?

We have come to the end of 'generational' or 'biological' growth whereby children of Christian parents, through the processes of baptism, Sunday school, and confirmation provide for a future church membership. Personal religion in the future will be based not on ethnicity or upbringing but on individual personal 'decision'.[12] All this suggests that we have to prioritize the making of new Christians for a new type of church in Britain. This will not be easy.

The one form of 'solid church' largely immune from secular pressures is the cathedral. Cathedrals have become focal points for a return to church. Over the past 11 years, average weekly attendance has risen by 43%. In a consumer culture where people travel to shop or be entertained, seekers of 'spirituality' will be drawn to the cathedrals because of the quality of the music, the ambiance but also because no firm personal commitment will be demanded of them.

Some 'emerging churches' or 'fresh expressions' also show evidence of numerical growth'. Although 25% of the members of 'fresh expressions' are already church-going Christians, 40% have never attended church before.[13] Jackson lists some features of successful 'fresh expressions'.

> focus on children and young families;
> work in schools and messy church;
> discipleship courses;
> lay leadership;
> Bible study and prayer;
> changing the times and location of services;
> deploying more clergy in the local community.

Jackson thinks that families and children are the most responsive 'fields' for evangelization.[14]

Do these new attendees contribute financially to the maintenance and support of the church? In most cases it is the 'grey headed' within 'traditional church' who resource 'fresh expressions'. They are prepared to do so because they hope these new Christians will move across to 'save' their own church by becoming members and office bearers. Given the present dynamic this is unlikely to happen.

An ecumenical dream.

There and Here

A main driver of the ecumenical dream was the desire to realize the prayer of Jesus 'that they may be one as we are one so that the world might believe'. It led to the Lund principle that 'we should not do anything apart which we could do together'. Mission, ecumenism and co-operation belong together. Given the World Wars of the 20th century, it can be seen as an attempt to capture the Ephesian vision of a world without walls – an '*oikos*' (one of the Greek words for 'house'). You may recall that the word 'ecumenical' comes from this.

The last century is littered with glitches and false starts. Attempts to achieve organic union have proved to be costly in time and energy. Problems with buildings, local loyalties, theological cussedness, issues of identity and power have haunted ecumenical activity. Ecclesiastical mergers, it has been suggested, instead of enabling growth have quickened decline.[15] Some advocates of ecumenism believed that renewal would come when the traditional churches accepted each other and pooled their resources. This has proved to be a fantasy.

Many Local Ecumenical Partnerships, once thought to be in the vanguard of the 'future great church' are either acting largely independent of their parent communions or suffocating under a blanket of ecclesiastical red-tape. The 20th-century ecumenical dream, according to Alister McGrath, has 'become the last refuge of the theological

There and Here

bore'.[16] Panic, at falling numbers, by leaders of Britain's mainline churches has driven ecumenism to the bottom of the ecclesiastical agenda.

The Ephesian vision with it ecumenical dimension looks not so much at the Church but at the work of the Spirit in the world. The central ecumenical question of the last century seems to have been: 'how can we demonstrate visible unity between diverse and divided churches?' This question is now compounded by further problems. Issues about sexuality and patriarchy are starting to fragment the main parent communions. Abuse scandals, particularly in the Roman Catholic Church, are distorting the ecumenical agenda. Finally we are coming to recognize that the 20th-century ecumenical agenda no longer works because its liberal assumptions are unacceptable to growing conservative evangelical churches.

The key ecumenical question for churches in Babylon should now be 'how can we together as churches celebrate and demonstrate justice, unity and diversity for people everywhere and also protect the planet?' This is more realistic because Christianity, out of all the world faiths, supposedly exhibits more cultural diversity than any other religion.[17] The following are examples of a new ecumenism.

1. On 2nd July 2005, as G8 leaders met in Scotland, a tidal wave of 225,000 marchers

There and Here

swept through the streets of Edinburgh in a never-ending flow, whistling, drumming, singing and chanting. This was a good natured advocacy of Make Poverty History. I was there as President of the Methodist Church and able to have conversation with Gordon Brown and Alistair Darling. The whole event, which had a carnival atmosphere, was multi-faith and multi-cultural. It was an ecumenical event; global, post-denominational and post-Christian.

2. Since then we have seen many local examples of practical ecumenism like the 'food banks' and the *Faith Works* 'sleep safe' projects. These have been prompted by the growing plight of the poor and homeless. 'Street Pastors' is another ecumenical project, this time attempting to help distressed teenagers caught up in the 'clubbing culture'.

3. Inderjit Bhogal, a former President of the Methodist Church, has proposed the setting up of Cities of Refuge (Numbers 35:6–34) where churches, synagogues, mosques, and gurdwaras provide sanctuary, safety and hospitality to vulnerable people fleeing from wars and conflicts.[18]

4. The original derelict Methodist chapel in Tolpuddle, Dorset, has been purchased to be imaginatively renovated. It was here in the early 1830s that some of the Tolpuddle martyrs worshipped. The majority of the six who were arrested, tried and deported for setting up a

There and Here

'union' were Methodists; at least two were local preachers.[19] This is an important heritage place marking the beginnings of the Trades Union Movement. Every year Union representatives from all over the UK and beyond process through the village with banners from Festival Field. The occasion ends with speeches and a stirring address. This ecumenical vision in Tolpuddle embraces Christianity, Trade Unionism, people of faith and of no faith.

What of the future of the Church in Britain?

In a world awash with fear and division Christians must address the growing gap between rich and poor. We must practise hospitality and seek justice for the planet and for all its peoples. Rowan Williams catches the Ephesian vision in one of his definitions of Church.

> The Church is first of all a kind of space cleared by God through Jesus in which people may become what God made them to be (God's sons and daughters). What we have to do about the Church is not to organize it as a society but to inhabit it as a climate or a landscape. It is a place where we can see properly – God, God's creation, ourselves. It is a place or dimension in the universe that is in some way growing towards being the universe itself in a restored relation-

ship with God. It is a place we are invited to enter, the place occupied by Christ, who is himself the climate and atmosphere of a renewed universe.[20]

NOTES

1. Timothy Keller, *Making Sense of God: An Invitation to the Skeptical*, H&S, 2016, p.26.
2. Keller, p.26.
3. Philip Jenkins, *The Next Christendom: The Coming of Global Christianity*, Oxford, 2002, pp.3f.
4. Much has been written about God being on the side of the poor, some of it questionable arising from misreadings of Matthew 25. One of the more satisfactory explanations comes from Michael Taylor, one time Director of Christian Aid. Reflecting on how in the ministry of Jesus the poor heard him gladly he comments 'God puts the poor first because they have not heard good-news for a long time' (Michael Taylor, *Good News for the Poor*, Mowbray, 1990, p.19).
5. Some will not be happy with the term 'self-sacrifice because of its association with 'gender oppression'. Furthermore the word 'sacrifice' went out of favour after the bloody sacrifices of the First World War. In my book *The Wrath of God Satisfied?* I have tried to show that the word is central to the atoning work of Christ and should therefore not be abandoned but redeemed. The idea of sacrifice will

There and Here

appear again in the final chapter where we are called upon 'to make the sacrifice complete'.
6. John V. Taylor, *The Go-Between God*, SCM Press, 1972, p.5.
7. Callum Brown, *The Death of Christian Britain*, London & New York: Routledge, 2001.
8. Callum Brown's analysis has flaws in it. For example it can be argued that the feminization of religion really began back in the 13th century (St Francis and St Clare). Further he seems not to take account of the thesis that 'gender identity' is to some extent a 'social construct'.
9. Michael Riddell, *Threshold of the Future*, London: SPCK, 1997, p.57.
10. Riddell, p.13.
11. Martyn Atkins, *Resourcing Renewal*, Inspire, 2007, p.62.
12. Keller, p.26.
13. Bob Jackson, *What Makes Churches Grow?* Church House Publishing, 2015, pp.45, 67.
14. Jackson, p.150.
15. Tom Stuckey, 'Mission and Ecclesiastical Collaboration', in Roger Standing, *As a Fire by Burning*, SCM Press, 2013, p.149.
16. Alister McGrath, *The Future of Christianity*, Oxford: Blackwell Publishers, 2002, p.85.
17. Over 90% of Muslims live in a band from Southeast Asian to the Middle East and Northern Africa. Over 95% of all Hindus are in India and its immediate environs. Some 88% of Buddhists are in East Asia. Looking at Christianity we find that there are

There and Here

sizeable number in Europe, the Americas, Africa, and Asia. (Keller, *Making Sense of God*, p.148)
18. www.cityofsanctuary.org
19. Although the 'Friendly Society for Agricultural Workers' was legal, their secret oath of allegiance was not. The court however wrongly relied on an inappropriate law and the new zealous judge wished to appease local landowners who were fearful lest the horrors of the French Revolution crossed the channel. Eventually after mass demonstrations and lobbying, pardons were given. George and James Loveless, Thomas and John Stanfield, and James Brine returned to England in 1837. James Hammett returned later. He was the only one to stay in Tolpuddle. He became a building labourer.
20. 'The Christian Priest Today' (slightly changed) on www.archbishopofcanterbury.org/1185.

5

THE BABYLONIAN CAPTIVITY OF THE CHURCH

I have been very zealous for the Lord, the God of hosts; for the Israelites have forsaken your covenant . . . I alone am left . . . Then the Lord said to him, 'Go return on our way to the wilderness of Damascus . . . I will leave seven thousand in Israel, all the knees that have not bowed to Baal. (1 Kings 19.14–15, 18)

Mission-Shaped Church was published in 2004. By the time I became President it had sold 16,000 copies. Although reflecting some of the content of my Presidential address (Appendix) it assumed Anglican privilege totally ignoring the existence of Methodism and all the other churches in Britain. John Hull gives a devastating critique. 'We looked for a mission-shaped church but what we found was a church-shaped mission.'[1]

The mission of God

John Hull's comment could equally be true of the Methodist Church since we still think of mission as something the Church does. Nearly seventy years ago this popular notion was turned on its head. Mission, argued Karl Barth, is not 'ours' it's 'God's'.[2] *Missio Dei* is the theological foundation for the church's mission and should be a replication of a dynamic understanding of Trinity.[3]

There have been many attempts since then to name the actual components of mission. The old formula of 'witness, fellowship, service and proclamation' has been discussed endlessly. Its limitations are now generally recognized.[4] John Hull has set out 'five marks' of Christian mission.

> To proclaim the good news of the kingdom of God
> To teach, baptize and nurture new believers
> To respond to human need by loving service
> To seek to transform unjust structures of society
> To strive to safeguard the integrity of creation and to sustain the life of the earth.

While most local churches go for the first three; the last two which relate to the wider world are more difficult.[5] In Chapter 2, I set out four dimensions of growth: *numerical, conceptual, organic* and *incarnational*. The Ephesian Christians, I said, were stuck in an 'adolescent phase' because they lacked *conceptual* growth. I also suggested that *incarnational* growth, where a church works for justice alongside the powerless, is paramount. Alan Padgett, writing from a Methodist perspective, says 'numerical growth is only healthy when it is accompanied by growth in other areas of spirituality namely 'outreach, biblical and theological depth, and the struggle for peace and justice'.[6]

Unfortunately seeking justice for people and the environment is at the bottom of the agenda of most churches. Could it be that the culture of Babylon has so permeated and compromised the Church that it has 'darkened our understanding' (Eph. 4.18)? We cannot confront the sins of Babylon without confronting ourselves; it would be like biting the hand that feeds us. The easy option is to let justice issues slip from our minds.

Robin Gill, examining the British scene in 1988, uncovered evidence of how large churches ignored smaller ones. He suggested that when churches of middle-class people appear to be successful they often lose their capacity to identify with those at the margins.[7] While there may be some truth in this, evidence today particularly from the 'black churches' suggest that many large churches not only have the resources to develop programmes of compassion for those at the margins but are not slow in enacting them. Justice however may still be another matter!

While Luke does a lot of counting, Paul does not. He commends the Thessalonian Christians not because of their increase in numbers but because they have retained their integrity through suffering, becoming 'imitators of us and of the Lord' (1 Thes.

1.6). For Paul numbers are not as significant as we might suppose.

Shopping for religion

In modern Babylon, 'religion' is an 'object of consumption' rather than 'a form of obligation'. Put simply, people will attend a church as long as it gives them what they want.[8] In a sensual culture like ours people are looking for a 'feel good' factor.

Reflect for a moment on the parable of the sower.[9] Unlike the receptive 'global fields' of churches in a culture of 'self-sacrifice', our Babylonian culture is littered with the hard stones of secularism, self-assertion and the suffocating weeds of consumerism. The 'seed of the Word' is also snatched away by the swooping rapidity of our ever accelerating pace of life. It is extremely difficult to reap a harvest in such a field. Some churches do appear to be growing but this is often due to families with young children by-passing a church of the 'grey headed' and 'choosing' to settle in a church with families like their own. Growth in many of the 'new churches' also occurs because dissatisfied Christians from the traditional churches 'shop-around' for a more lively church. In parts of London and in cities elsewhere there is often a large Anglican or Baptist Church which has embraced a more charismatic style of worship. Such churches tend to 'hoover up' young families and young people from all around. Membership growth here therefore precipitates a membership collapse elsewhere in an overall saga of decline.

Pete Ward helps us to further understand this.[10] He observes that Western culture is becoming more and more fluid. Technological innovation is occurring at such an alarming rate that change is the name of the game. Hitherto, modernity substituted one solid institution and set of values for another. Now modernity itself is undergoing a liquefying process making everything flexible, fuzzy and subject to obsolescence. Our liquid culture has undermined the time-honoured values of loyalty to place, tradition and denomination. If church is to connect with a 'liquid culture' then it too must become 'liquid'. Traditional church, by remaining 'solid', has acquired all the features of a heritage site and a refuge for an ageing nostalgic community.

The notion of 'membership' in a consumer society of 'choice' becomes problematic. Members belong to a static organization; disciples lives with uncertainty. Membership focuses on church; discipleship anticipates the Kingdom of God. Membership values faithfulness; discipleship requires faith. Leaving cathedrals and certain historic churches on one side for the moment (but not forgetting them), it is argued that we must give priority to 'emerging church' if 'inherited church' is to reconnect with contemporary culture. A word of warning however! 'Fresh expressions' or 'emerging churches' should not be regarded as the answer to our present difficulties.

Embedded in the human condition as 'negatives' are the dark side of church which will persist in 'fresh expressions', although this will not be evident until the honeymoon period is over.[11]

Does the secular 'god of the market' deliver happiness? Some people today, experiencing the emptiness of mammon, are genuinely searching for 'something' which was once here but has evaporated. Memory, nostalgia, utopian ideas of the past; these can be important 'motivators' giving churches, suitably tuned in, the opportunity of making new Christians. In this the cathedrals and other heritage buildings have an advantage.

Christians coming from other parts of the world can not only boost our numbers but bring a new vitality to our faith and worship. Some will join the congregation of 'inherited church'. Others will seek a place of their own where they are able to give expression to their traditions of Christian worship and identity. Will this inflow cease in a post Brexit church?

We live in uncertain apocalyptic times. Fear can often prompt individuals to turn to religion for comfort and meaning. This again raises questions about 'religious consumerism'. Some of our churches are providing a 'feel good' factor for their congregations but are they also making genuine Christians disciples prepared to embrace not just a few but all five of the mission marks listed above?

Word and words

Babylon is a noisy place seducing us with its images and technology. The Whore of Babylon dazzles our eyes enticing us to gaze at her with desire and lust. She encourages us to be self-obsessed. 'I want people to look at me, contact me, think good of me and give me an assurance that I am still a living person.' Why this fretful need to check our phones constantly and drip feed ourselves with tweets, jokes and instagrams? Can we no longer appreciate an historic building or a beautiful scene without plastering a selfie right across it? What about our eating habits? A gnawing anxiety comes upon some people when they have nothing to occupy their jaws either by eating or by spilling empty verbiage onto others? Words and noise are the background music of a consumer society. We have forgotten that only in stillness can the human spirit expand and flower.

Babylon has invaded the worship of some of our churches, 'inherited' as well as 'emerging'. It is argued that people today have a short attention span so we need to adapt worship to retain people's interest. Boredom has become the enemy so fill the time with image, song, visuals, clips, chat and a short snappy address. The temptation to entertain and pacify is powerful. The worshippers have become a consumer audience.

From a theological perspective who is the real audience in worship? God is the audience. The congregation is the cast of performers. The worship leaders are the producers and stage managers. Worship does not exist to entertain, educate or teach a congregation. Worship exists for the praise of God. The glorious opening chapter of Ephesians sets illumination within the context of praise and prayer. Of course there is a paradox here because God is both the One worshipped and also the One who, through his Holy Spirit, generates worship in a congregation.

How do we encourage members of the congregation to become performers and participate corporately? Some churches compound the dumbing-down of worship with kinder garden activities. 'I'm fed up with receiving paper and pencil, told to write something down and share it with the person sitting next to me' is a comment I hear far too often. 'We are being talked down to and treated like children' is another comment. Churches that have absorbed Babylon into their worship mistake activity for participation and responsiveness for depth.

Barbara Brown Taylor, in *When God is Silent*, tells how she listened to an Easter sermon in which a large expectant congregation was told bunny jokes; one after another. Finally the preacher said 'Easter was God's big joke so we should have a good laugh'. Taylor ends: 'I wanted someone with a badge to go up and arrest that guy.'[12]

The Willow Creek Community Church in a series of surveys rolled out across thousands of churches in the rich Western World revealed some alarming news about preaching.[13]

- Over half the people who desire life-changing Bible teaching do not get it.
- Preaching is boring 54% of Christians.
- Of the 72% of people who want preaching with depth, only 19% were getting it.

Taylor concludes that our frenetic lives, our technology, the proliferation of words and the cacophony of sound has not only drowned out the Word of God but that God himself has withdrawn into the Silence. She points to the prophet Isaiah who passes a terrible indictment on worship in the Jerusalem temple. 'God says when you stretch out your hands I will hide my eyes from you; even though you make many prayers I will not listen' (Isa. 1.15).

Spiritual and theological emptiness is not only found in worship but in the actions and strategies of some ordained ministers and priests. Here is the minister who having moved to a new place proceeds to implement some scheme or model of mission which, because it had worked in the previous situation, is assumed to work here. This is the action of a mechanic rather than a priest. A similar thing is taking place when members of a congregation visit another church which they perceive to be 'successful' and then return to their own church with the message 'we should be doing that here.'

These are quick-fit structural solutions. *Conceptual growth* will not occur since these bypass the difficult theological activity of listening, praying, thinking and waiting on the Spirit. Is it any wonder that God may no longer listen to our prayers?

A heroic mission?

Paul's ministry and mission can be labelled 'heroic'. Pioneer leaders of emerging churches sometimes copy this model. Some are larger than life personalities and can operate successfully in pre-modern and modern contexts where authority is still recognized and acknowledged. In our post-modern celebrity culture where image has replaced authority can heroic ministry make a lasting impact?

The passage from 1 Kings 19, heading this chapter, describes Elijah's state of mind after Mount Carmel. An epic battle had taken place between himself and a 'Babylon type culture' represented by Jezebel and the prophets of Baal. Elijah's exhausting day ends with him climbing a mountain, praying for rain and running seventeen miles to Jezreel. A nervous breakdown is to be expected! The symptoms are described; fear and flight, the abandoning of his companion, lack of appetite, paranoia and whining self-pity.

Ian Cowley in his book *The Contemplative Minister* says:

> there was a time when the Christian ministry offered the opportunity to spend a life time in prayer, study, preparing, delivering and exercising faithful care in the community. Not so now. The job requires 'a heroic combination of stamina, multi-tasking and change management'.[14]

Yvonne Warren in her survey of Anglican clergy in two dioceses says: 'Guilt is often a major preoccupation for clergy. They feel that they have "let God down" . . . they can never get it right or do enough.'[15] Ministers today who embrace the 'heroic' risk 'burn out' or 'breakdown'.

Christina Maslach in her studies of 'burnout' suggests this is often caused not by personal inadequacy but by the organization's 'structural stressing'.[16] It used to be supposed that advanced information technology would give people more time to do the things that really matter. According to

Maslach the opposite has happened. We are still expected to do what we always did but now have the additional task of responding to and producing organizational data for the technological machines we have created. The end result is we now have less time than we had before.

In spite of Elijah's spectacular fireworks on Carmel, little was achieved. The principalities and powers of Babylon simply regrouped. The same is true today. Amazing twitter sound-bites astonish but do they move things forward? Donald Trump, in the spirit of Babylon, has adopted this mode of communication for his Presidency.

John the Baptist was thought to be a reincarnation of Elijah. His heroic re-enactment of the Mount Carmel style of ministry led to his imprisonment. In an 'Elijah type' depression he questions his own vocation. John, for all his greatness has become least in the kingdom of God (Lk. 7.28). The future of the Church in Britain will not be determined through spectacular events of earthquake, wind and fire but by something much less obvious – silence – a gentle whispering sound.

A Babylonian captivity

I have taken the title for this chapter from a pamphlet Martin Luther wrote in October 1520. In it he attacked 'indulgences'. These were bits of paper telling you that your sins were forgiven.

Luther called these tickets to heaven 'A swindlers trick of the Roman Flatterers'.[17] They were sold to enhance the glory of the papacy by raising money for the building of St Peter's. They were expressions of 'cheap grace'.[18] They gave people a 'feel good' experience without requiring discipleship. Luther's pamphlet attacked the seven sacraments which had become an ecclesiastical control system. Luther did not explicitly say this but would do so later.

The features of Babylon were there in the Roman Church of the 16th century: money, power, control, image, centralization and glory. Of the five marks of mission, with which this chapter began, Luther was in effect going straight to number four 'to transform the unjust structures of society'. Against the glory of the Church, Luther set up a theology of the cross.

The Church in Britain has fallen under the thrall of a new Babylon. What should we do? *Mission-Shaped Church* spelt it out for Anglicans. 'The stark reality of this situation should be a cause for profound repentance and renewed missionary endeavour.'[19] Is God saying something similar to the Methodist Church?

NOTES

1. John Hull, *Mission-Shaped Church: A Theo-logical Response*, SCM Press, 2006, p.36.
2. J. Verkyl, *Contemporary Missiology*, Grand Rapids,

MI: Eerdmans, 1978, p.3.
3. Thomas Thangaraj, *The Common Task: A Theology of Christian Mission*, Nashville: Abingdon Press, 1999, p.38.
4. Tom Stuckey, *Into the Far Country. A Theology of Mission for an Age of Violence*, Epworth, 2003, pp.128–129.
5. These marks were taught by John Hull within the Queen's Foundation for Ecumenical Theological Education in Birmingham. A Prophetic Church Committee, was set up to encourage marks four and five; the resisting of unjust structures and caring for the environment.
6. Alan Padgett, 'The Church Growth Movement: A Wesleyan Critique', in *The Mission of the Church in the Methodist Perspective*, Lampeter: Edwin Mellen Press, 1992, p.141.
7. Robin Gill, *Beyond Decline*, SCM Press Ltd, 1988, p.80.
8. Grace Davie, 'From Obligation to Consumption', essay in Steven Croft (ed.), *The Future of the Parish System*, Church House Publishing, 2006, pp.42ff.
9. Donald McGavran, *Understanding Church Growth*, Grand Rapids, MI: Eerdmans, 1970, pp.245–248.
10. Pete Ward, *Liquid Church*, Carlisle: Paternoster Press, 2002.
11. Sara Savage, 'On the analysist's couch', in Steven Croft (ed.), p.30.
12. Barbara Brown Taylor, *When God is Silent*, Canterbury Press, 2013.

13. Chris Green, *Cutting to the Heart: Applying the Bible in Teaching and Preaching*, IVP, 2015, p.94.
14. Ian Cowley, *The Contemplative Minister*, Bible Reading Fellowship, 2015, p.11.
15. Yvonne Warren, *The Cracked Pot: The State of Today's Anglican Clergy*, Kevin Mayhew, 2002, p.54.
16. Christina Maslach, *Burnout*, Malor: ISHK, 2003, p.69.
17. Martin Luther (trans. A Steinhaeuser), *The Babylonian Captivity of the Church*, Cross Reach Pub., 2017.
18. 'Cheap grace is the deadly enemy of the Church . . . Cheap grace means grace sold on the market like cheapjack's wares. The sacraments, the forgiveness of sin, and the consolations of religion are thrown away at cut prices.' (Dietrich Bonhoeffer, *The Cost of Discipleship*, SCM, 1959, p.35.)
19. *Mission-Shaped Church*, Church of England Publishing, 2004, p.39.

6

METHODISM: WHERE ARE YOU?

To the angel of the church in Ephesus ... I know your work, your toil and your patient endurance. I know you cannot tolerate evildoers ... and that you have not grown weary. But I have this against you, you have abandoned the love you had at first. Remember then from what you have fallen; repent, and do the works you did at first ... Let anyone who has an ear listen to what the Spirit is saying to the churches. (Rev. 2.1–7)

As a passenger on the good ship *Methodist Connexion*, I wonder where we are heading. I view with concern the activities of the officers and crew, many of whom are severely overworked. I realize that even as a retired minister in the Southampton District I am not meant to be relaxing on a luxury cruise liner heading for sunny shores. Neither do I believe that I am on the Titanic as it ploughs through dangerous waters. But this is not all! I am worried about the passengers. Many are no longer enjoying the trip while quite a few of the younger families have fallen overboard or disembarked.

The Ephesian commendation

In the Revelation passage which heads this chapter there is a commendation but it is followed by a condemnation. In spite of past difficulties the Ephesian Church remains. They have dealt with the evil within[1] and are praised for their faithfulness, their endurance and their determination to keep going. These positive affirmations readily apply to our Methodist Church when I think of the continuing sacrificial commitment of our members.

Fresh expressions

The Methodist Church in Britain is to be commended for taking up, with some enthusiasm, the idea of 'fresh expressions of church'.[2] Our favourite forms are probably 'messy church', 'café church' and 'godly play'.[3] When originally conceived I had understood 'fresh expressions' to be about planting a radically different type of church, located in a secular building with a worship style shaped to attract. I had in mind Paul's decision in Acts 19 to leave the synagogue and hire neutral premises so that 'outsiders' who became Christians would not be intimidated by the traditions of the 'insiders'. By and large we have not taken that route.[4] Although there are some more radical examples most of our 'fresh expressions' occur within our own buildings.[5] Martyn Atkins, as President in 2007, maintained that 'fresh expressions' thrive because they have a much more limited focus than 'inherited church'. They go for excellence in what they do and operate with a greater degree of vulnerability and honesty.[6]

Often linked with 'fresh expressions' is 'pioneer ministry'. Methodism has started to recognize that there are some presbyters and deacons within our ranks who have a real gift for church planting. Most are stationed within our normal matching process.[7] Some, however, are finding their 'pioneer' vocation' constrained because of circuit demands. There are also lay persons able to exercise this ministry but our systems are not always flexible enough to accommodate them. Although we are taking 'fresh expression' initiatives they are happening at a much slower rate than in the Church of England.

Social holiness

Methodists are to be commended for continuing to upgrade their buildings and offering them for use by outsiders.[8] Over many decades this 'community use' service function has been a primary expression of Methodist mission. It has made a huge and often underestimated contribution to the social capital and cohesion of local communities. Methodism has a long history of appointing deacons, presbyters and lay persons as chaplains. Most circuit ministers have some involvement in schools or other community institutions. A few are completely released from circuit responsibilities to work in a specified area of need within the community. If we think of 'church growth' in the terms described in Chapter 2 by Orlando Costas, then of the four ingredients of numerical, conceptual, organic and incarnational, we probably score high on the latter. Methodists want to demonstrate Christ's love for the neighbour.

Grass roots lay members of the Methodist Church, almost without exception, get involved with people and organizations which have little or nothing to do with church. Some become local councillors. Some join pressure groups. Others staff charity shops and food banks. This desire to help others is in our bloodstream. One senses that even if our worship attendance is dwindling, the Methodist social ethic will endure.

Incredible money raisers

'Earn all you can; save all you can; give all you can' is one of Wesley's enduring legacies,[9] remembered by many because the last of these three injunctions was conveniently forgotten by Margaret Thatcher in one of her speeches. The Methodist people are incredible money raisers. Although this is particularly so in relation to their own local church building projects this generosity is extended to needy people beyond our shores.

The Methodist World Mission Fund, in various partnership schemes, supports projects and individuals right across the world. Within the umbrella of the Methodist Church are parallel organizations also with focused giving. Methodist Women in Britain (once called 'Network) contributes generously and prayerfully. 'All we can' once called the 'The Methodist Relief and Development Fund' (MRDF) is another umbrella organization which exists to help people in the world's poorest communities not just with emergency relief but in long-term development, education and fighting poverty. All of these, and many others, have their advocates at the grass-roots. Millions of pounds flow from local Methodist churches through these conduits giving expression to Methodism's global mission

Joyful hospitality

The hymn 'All are Welcome' is an appropriate addition to our hymnody. Methodism has a strong tradition of providing hospitality and giving a warm welcome to all.[10] A visitor entering a Methodist Church on Sunday will, in nearly every case, be greeted with smiles. We are a hospitable people and want that person to come to our church again. Such activities retain the tradition of Wesley's 'warm heart' and can generate a 'feel good' factor in others. On the whole we are a 'happy people'.

In Babylon   Happiness comes from retail therapy.
In Methodism Happiness comes from helping others.

Being a global Church we have a particularly fondness for Methodists who come to us from other parts of the world. We are more than grateful for their presence and for what they bring to us. There are an increasing number of instances of Methodists going the 'second mile' in providing hospitality for strangers, migrants, asylum seekers and those fleeing war and persecution. Trying to do 'all the good we can' is part of our Wesleyan heritage.

The Methodist Church remains the fourth largest denomination in Britain. According to the November 2016 statistics, some 210,000 people are attending our church services each week. Eight in every thousand people in Britain are being visited, welcomed, cared and prayed for according to our Community Roll figures. We are taking up many of the mission opportunities described in Chapter 4 and in spite of our ageing profile we continue to punch above our weight.

The Ephesian condemnation.

In the past ten years our membership has decreased by a third from 304,971 in 2003 to

208,738 in 2013. During the same period the number of children attending worship has fallen by 58%. More recent figures reveal an even more drastic drop in membership. With no substantial influx of younger families our age profile continues to rise. Faithful officers who have valiantly served the church for years are giving up because of age or failing health. It is becoming more and more difficult getting new volunteers. Numbers, however, in London and other large conurbations are holding up mainly because of the arrival of Methodists from other parts of the world. Numerical growth here has more to do with 'transfers in' than with 'conversions'. In 1932, the year of Methodist Union, our membership was 838,019. It is now around 188,000. As with all the other traditional churches in Britain, Babylon and death are taking their toll.

The age of our congregations place an added load on our ministers. Even with an effective system of pastoral care the ever increasing demands for visiting the sick and the dying consume inordinate amounts of time. Many superintendents find themselves caught up in a plethora of meetings. Some chairs of district (our equivalent to Anglican bishops) have to deal with increasing numbers of complaints – a feature of our 'self-assertive' culture.

The pull of the past

For ageing congregations, their local buildings and traditions hold such powerful associations that they resist any change. Like some rail passengers they prefer to travel with their backs to the future. In their longing for the halcyon days of full churches, they try to maintain the fading programmes of the past and become increasingly depressed as fewer and fewer people attend. There have been many instances over the last twenty years of influential office holders clinging to power and thus shutting out new opportunities. Their church has ceased to be church and become a 'nostalgic religious club'.[11] Martyn Atkins comments:

> Change in inherited church is born of desperation. Change is accepted when there is no other option, like deciding to leave the house and get into the boat as the water reaches your neck . . . Equally, some readiness to change is born of exhaustion; so many local Christians in inherited church are simply weary with it all.[12]

Alongside the poor?

John Wesley's proclamation to the miners of Bristol on 2nd April 1739 was an exposition of Luke 4.18. 'The Spirit of God is upon me because he has anointed me to preach good news to the poor . . .' Charles sets this to music.

The poor, as Jesus' bosom-friends,

Methodism: Where Are You?

The poor he makes his latest care,
To all his successors commends,
And wills us on our hands to bear:
The poor our dearest care we make,
Aspiring to superior bliss,
And cherish for their Saviour's sake,
And love them with a love like his.[13]

The Methodist priority for the poor arose not from charity, nor a sense of duty and not even from a desire for social justice. It sprung, as it did for the Franciscans, from a discipleship vocation to be 'imitators of Christ'. Early Methodist theology was fully incarnational. Wesley understood this not as *serving the poor*, but as *living with the poor*.[14] He wove this identification into his model of holiness. As Methodism grew and became more middle class this identification was lost. Methodism in Britain (as in the US) thus relinquished its original identity.

The needs of the poor in Britain are as desperate as ever. The Conference of 2016 however took a retrograde step which, according to John Howard, demonstrates that it has forgotten all about the theology of our 'Mission Alongside the Poor Programme' (MAPP) and failed to grasp the significance of 'alongside' with its incarnational theology.[15] I suspect that where Methodism is growing, in other parts of the world, it does operate 'alongside the poor' in a mutual relationship of learning and serving. I am reminded of Theodore

Jennings' stinging indictment of Methodist Churches which forget this theology.

> Methodism was conceived as a call to scriptural holiness. Holiness means the imitation of the divine love which comes to us without worldly power and influence to dwell with us in a radical solidarity and sacrificial generosity. Without this love for the least, all our 'church growth' strategies lead to apostasy. Without the holiness of solidarity with the poor and despised all our evangelization will only produce conversions to religious paganism. Unless we offer a radical alternative to the middle-class life style we will be but a religious reflection of the world that is perishing. No, Methodism will not cease to exist. But unless we look beyond mere symptoms of what Wesley diagnosed as the underlying malady we will only be building larger and fancier sepulchres for a 'dead sect, having the form of religion but without the power'.[16]

Structural strangulation

While we may be falling short in the test of 'incarnational growth', we are failing completely in 'organic growth'. Our Connexional system has atrophied into a grinding bureaucratic machine. Martin Percy looking in at British Methodism is puzzled by our heavy organizational baggage and

Methodism: Where Are You?

ecclesiastical civil service. He comments that 'our bureaucracy is stifling our democracy and democracy has triumphed over theocracy'.[17]

The mission of God the Trinity is to generate diversity.[18] Babylon's mission is to centralize power, micromanage, and produce 'sameness'. Diversity and creativity are signs of organic growth. Connexionalism was once an imaginative theological representation of Catholicity in a growing church. Its grinding wheels have now become an impediment to growth.[19] This drive towards centralization is relentless.[20] Although this may be true, the 'average' Methodist has little idea about our organizational structures. Local churches by and large just get on with it.

We like mechanical and practical solutions as we turn ourselves into a public utility for the 'religious and social consumer'. Over the past couple of decades we have been shifting the furniture of worship; chairs not pews, power-point for hymn books, a music group rather than an organ. Inordinate amounts of time and money plus thousands of meetings have been required to effect these changes. This is Babylon at work amongst us.

The way in which structural solutions are implemented is as important as the change itself. Mission is relational both in its substance and in its implementation. Although done with the intention of securing the future, insensitive imposition can precipitate a haemorrhaging of the very people we can least afford to lose. Pursuing structural solutions in any case often leads to more meetings, stress, exhaustion and illness rather than blessing.[21] Ministers are not called to save the church but to love, teach and demonstrate the salvation of God. In a Babylonian culture, structure, power and appropriate image are first required before a consumer mission can be launched. Methodism has tended to go down this route. In a church led by the Spirit, structures do not precede mission, they follow it.

One of the few growing circuits in the Southampton District has only one ordained minister. The circuit has an evangelical tradition. Lay leaders have not only caught the Spirit but are operating with faith and imagination. All the traditional tasks expected of a superintendent in such a demanding situation are not easily done but oversight is essential. Most months the superintendent is approached by some group from one of the churches who want to initiate an event. He has devised four questions which have to be considered: Is it legal? Is it heretical? Is it divisive? Is it missional? If these are answered satisfactorily the event goes ahead.

Long in organization but short in theology[22]

Gareth Powell, Secretary of the Conference, says that there is 'no shortage of interest and

Methodism: Where Are You?

enthusiasm for the people called Methodists to talk about God but whether we know how to do it is a different matter'.[23]

This is our Achilles heel. We have thousands of outsiders on our premises each week. Huge opportunities for relationship building and conversation exist but I see little evidence of us engaging in forms of verbal witness. In focusing on structure, ministry, presence and social witness we have allowed 'verbal witness' to escape.[24]

Confidence and the ability to speak about God arises from 'theology'. A Russian priest once said 'if you want to learn theology, go to the liturgy not the library'.[25] While Anglicans carry their theology in their liturgy, we have traditionally carried ours in our hymns. It has been argued however that the rich theology of our hymns/songs has increasingly been watered down.[26] As mentioned in the last chapter, the culture of Babylon can enter worship. To what extent has it entered ours? Going to a Methodist church on Sunday can provide a 'feel good' experience particularly if you find out in advance who is leading the worship. I do wonder, however, if this is created more by the 'fellowship' and chatting together after the benediction than by the worship experience itself? I think we have reversed the great commandment. Is this our Methodist take on it?

'The first commandment is, Thou shalt love thy neighbour as thyself,
the second is thus; thou shalt try to find God in this.'

The Ephesian Church was indicted because it had lost the love which once it had. We Methodists have a great love for our church and its fellowship. We may even love our committees and meetings. We certainly love to see our buildings used by the community. We love to do practical things. We still want to love our neighbour as ourselves but . . . !

NOTES

1. They had dealt with the Nicolaitans who also were a problem for the churches of Pergamum and Thyatira. Evidence is confused but the Nicolaitans may have been Christians who fused their Christianity with surrounding culture. Balaam, mentioned 2.14 was the father of religious syncretism (C. B. Caird, *The Revelation of St John the Divine*, Black, 1966). It seems that the Ephesian Church had managed to expel Babylon from it life.
2. David Gamble, who was President in 2009, tried to encourage fresh expressions to really enter our blood stream when he said, 'fresh expression isn't just about what the national team is going to do, but it's the job of every church, every minister,

every circuit to be considering the places where God is calling us to' (*Methodist Church website*, October, 2016).

3. It has been suggested that Messy Church is little more than a relabelling of some of the imaginative work we have traditionally done with toddler groups and families.

4. The 'STALL' (Salvation To ALL) has no premises. The main street in Christchurch, Dorset is closed to traffic on Mondays. Street traders set up their stalls and visitors come from miles around. One of our ministers set up a stall 18 months ago. His drawings get people interested, conversations follow, sometimes prayer. He is accepted by the other stall holders and exercises a ministry amongst them. He once celebrated communion. Such was the demand that this was repeated several times during the day. The 'Stall' is not a feeder activity for church. It is church.

5. Some new 'churches' of this type now exist like 'Tube Station, Cornwall'; 'The Beacon, Dartford'; 'Potters Church', Burslem Mission; and 'New Song Network Church'. There are other examples some more radical than others: Grace Church Hackney, Bread Church, the Boiler Room Community, Sanctus I, Manchester, Zac's Place, Cook@Chapel, Jazz Church in Birmingham, Safespace in Telford and LegacyXS. Very different is the Cable Street Community in Shadwell, East London and 'little church' in York which is a community formed for

those with profound addiction (some of these are described in Andrew Roberts, *Holy Habits*, MD Publishing, 2016). There are also the street-level 'alternative churches' described by John Vincent in *Methodism Unbound*, Church in the Market Place, 2015.
6. Martyn Atkins, *Resourcing Renewal. Shaping Churches for the Emerging Future*, Inspire, 2007, p.96.
7. Methodist Ministers are appointed to circuits through a 'stationing process'. A couple of 'connexional stationing matching' meetings are held every year in which each Methodist district is represented by a presbyter and lay-person. Those presbyters and deacons who have indicated that they wish to move circuit are 'matched', according to gifts and desires, to the vacancies available. With our ministerial shortage and the increasingly complex needs of ministers this 'jig saw' has in recent years become increasingly difficult. (Note that the system is far more complicated than I have indicated). John Taylor (a former President) has recently asked whether we ought not now to abandon this creaking system and move to a 'free market' economy where circuits and ministers advertise their needs as and when they arise. (A comment at a gathering of Past Presidents and Vice-Presidents of Conference on 19th January 2017.)
8. Good practical example of this is given by Reeves and Downer (*Methodist Recorder*, 17th March

2017). Sometimes a vacant manse is made available for asylum seekers.
9. Sermon XLIV – 'The Use of Money', *Wesley's Standard Sermons*, E. Sugden (ed.), Epworth, 1921.
10. This welcome for all comes from our Wesley's Arminian background and is perpetuated in the Methodist slogan 'All need to be saved, All can be saved, All can know themselves saved, All can be saved to the uttermost'.
11. Appendix 4:3.
12. Martin Atkins, ibid., p.66.
13. Ted Campbell, 'The Image of Christ in the Poor', found in Richard P. Heitzenrater (ed.), *The Poor and the People Called Methodists*, Kingswood Books, 2002, p.51.
14. Theodore Runyon, *The New Creation: John Wesley's Theology Today*, Nashville: Abingdon Press, 1998, p.185.
15. The *Mission Alongside the Poor* programme (MAPP) was launched in 1983. Some years later John Howard, me and others were members of a Connexional Group tasked to integrate MAPP into the total life of the Church. It changed the way we awarded grants but little else. Integration never happened. John Howard, 'Re-envisioning Mission Along-side the Poor', in John Vincent, *Methodism Abounding*, Church in the Market Place, 2016, pp.65f. The Conference 2014 changed the name of MAPP to Methodist Action on Poverty and Justice

(MAPJ).
16. Theodore Jennings Jr, 'Good News to the Poor in the Wesleyan Heritage', found in James Logan (ed.), *Theology and Evangelism in the Wesleyan Heritage*, Kingswood Books, 1994, p.156. What does this attack on 'middle-class' lifestyle mean in actual practice? Even in Heitzenrater's book (mentioned above) this is not clearly spelt out.
17. Martyn Percy, 'Back to the Future: A Search for a Thoroughly Modern Methodist Ecclesi-ology', found in C. Marsh, B. Beck, H. Wareing and A. Shier-Jones (eds), *Unmasking Methodist Theology*, Continuum, 2004, p.207.
18. In its doctrine of the Trinity, the Western Church emphasizes the one God who is revealed in three subsisting persons. A local preacher, who is to be congratulated for preaching on Trinity Sunday, told me how he explained the Trinity. He said 'I am father to my children, son to my parents and husband to my wife'. I suspect that most of us view the Trinity in this way and place emphasis on the one God – a single person rather than three persons in partnership and communion. Concentrating on oneness creates a static Church, keen to organize, centralize and control. Diversity and creativity is swallowed up in the drive for unity. (Appendix 2:1)

The early Greek theologians of the Eastern Church emphasized the distinctiveness of the persons of the Trinity. They use the word

perichoresis, which literally means 'to proceed about each other' to describe movement within the Trinity. There is a sort of barn dance; a flow and flux going on within God; a finding and a losing, a circling and spiralling of partners until all three are transfigured in each other, lost in a love-making out of which new universes are conceived and born (Appendix 2:2).
19. My Presidential address was interrupted by enthusiastic applause when I suggested that we shift power from the local church to the circuit meeting and give them the legal authority to close resistant churches, sell off the buildings and use the proceeds to employ and deploy staff in imaginative ways. See Appendix 4:4 and 4:5.
20. Peter Stephens writing in the *Methodist Recorder*, 28th October 2016.
21. Methodism has a predilection for organiz-ational overload. When things go wrong, particularly if we fear litigation, we produce new standing orders and sometimes additional structures. These can have a training scheme added. This is costly in time and money. Do we have a system where good intensions multiply structural stressing and operational overload?
22. These words were used by Gordon Rupp, a former President of the Conference, in his description of Methodism.
23. Reflections from the Secretary of the Conference to the 2016 Conference (7th July 2016).

24. The report *Time to Talk of God* gathers dust (Appendix 1:4).
25. Nicola Vidamour (*Methodist Recorder*, 31st March 2017).
26. Christine Stuckey, in her thesis *The Poetry of Perfection*, has shown in her examination of Methodist hymns how over the years the journey towards perfection/holiness has become secularized.

Part 3
PROPHECY

7

EXILE?

How shall we sing the Lord's song in a strange land? If I forget you, O Jerusalem, let my right hand wither! Let my tongue cleave to the roof of my mouth, if I do not remember you, if I do not set Jerusalem above my highest joy! (Ps. 137. 4–6)

Hardly any of the thousands of Jews transported and exiled by Nebuchadnezzar were to return to Jerusalem and when there was at last an opportunity to make the long trek back few did. The majority simply stayed on built houses, settled down, had children, got involved in commerce and absorbed Babylon into their system. Many put Jerusalem from their minds. Some remembered with nostalgic affection. Others tried to keep the faith alive trying to be in Babylon but not of Babylon. But there were a few who held on to the hope of a new Jerusalem and passed their dream on to their children.

The Church in Britain has absorbed Babylon into its system. But ours is a comfortable Babylon which has lulled us to sleep. This is not so for most Christians today. Across the world, from Nigeria to

Exile?

Vietnam, an estimated 200 million Christians face harassment, arrest, torture and death because of their faith. Christians are the most persecuted religious group in the world.[1] James Laney in a sermon about Christian identity in a comfortable Babylon says:

> When we look back at the history of the Church, every time we see that the Church has become captive to the dominant identity of its society, every time it has become comfortable with its role in culture, it has lost its universality. With the loss of universality, it has lost the power to create, not merely to evangelize, but also the power to become renewed.[2]

I have already mentioned that a huge paradigm shift is taking place. The old is passing and the new, though on its way, has yet to be revealed. It is a liminal moment for the inhabitants of Babylon. Brueggemann states that for Christians it is a time for *relinquishing and receiving*.

> The great moves that God is working in the public arena impinge upon every aspect of personal life. Relinquishment and reception . . . entails nothing less than dying in order to be raised to new life.[3]

In speaking of the Holy Spirit in Chapter 2, I wrote: 'He takes the responsibility for the filling; we through repentance have the responsibility for the emptying'. Luther, in confronting the Babylonian captivity of the Church, set the cross over and against the glory of the Church. Paul does the same in Corinth by pricking the bubble of the church's hubris.

> God chose what is foolish in the world to shame the wise; God chose what is weak in the world to shame the strong; God chose what is low and despised in the world, things that are not to reduce to nothing things that are. (1 Cor.1.27)

The future of the Church in Britain

1. The end of centralization

Alistair MacIntyre (mentioned in Chapter 3) suggests, that in order to preserve the values of truth in savage and uncertain times, we need a new Benedict. He was thinking of St Benedict, the hermit who lived in the 5th century. Although a layman, his influence is felt even to this day. He established a Rule for the monasteries which brought simplicity, common sense and practical wisdom. He wished them to be less autocratic, more gentle and hospitable. MacIntyre argues for the establishing of communities which will preserve the virtues of the past and become beacons of hope for the future.[4]

A few years before MacIntyre the Roman Catholic theologian Karl Rahner, looking at events in Latin

Exile?

America, Africa, Asia and parts of the United States, prophesied that the future church would not be centralized but dispersed in the form of scattered base communities. Local people, through free initiative and association, would in the power of the Spirit seek to engage with the issues of their place.

Robert Schreiter, following the same path, said that in response to the challenge of globalization, local churches should focus on 'the boundaries between those who profit from and enjoy the fruits of globalization and those who are excluded or oppressed by it'.[5]

Simon Jenkins in his *Short History of England* observes that change has only come about when the monolithic tendencies of rulers have been confronted by resurgent forces from below. He concludes that in Britain we are approaching the end of centralization.[6]

Phil Potter, one time Archbishops' Missioner, in his book *Pioneering a New Future*, takes his lead from the internet revolution and argues that we are starting to witness the demise of huge centralized organizations. He concludes that the Church must therefore 'decentralize'.[7] He recognizes the paradigm shift and tells us that we can no longer keep patching the old wineskins. The wineskins must now be abandoned.[8] The old paradigm was based on the model of attracting people in. The new paradigm must focus on the dispersed presence of

Christians in the community. 'The sacred space of the temple in Acts 2 has less significance than the actions and the networking of the small groups of Christians in the community who 'do little things in a big way'.[9]

In Chapter 1, I described the dynamic nature of the Trinity and how the Ephesian writer reworked the idea of monotheism. The Church in its theological story has struggled with where to put the emphasis in its understanding of Trinity. Should we focus on the unity of God or on the diversity of God as represented in the three persons?[10] We, in the West, have gone for the former.[11] Is this why the Western Church views mission in terms of 'centralizing' and 'gathering-in'? In the new paradigm with the advent of popularism and the call for devolution I suggest we need to view the Trinity in another way.

2. Smallness

Bevans and Schroeder, two Roman Catholic theologians, begin their huge book on mission with this remarkable sentence, 'One of the most important things Christians need to know about the Church is that the Church is not of ultimate importance'.[12] We in the West have compounded our difficulties in substituting 'church' for 'Spirit' as the third person of the Trinity. This has distorted both our view of mission and of church. The Church over the centuries ebbs and flows, comes

Exile?

and goes. The visible Church, as we have hitherto known it in Britain, can almost disappear but it will reappear in a different form in a different place at a different time. Luther describes this movement in an alarming way:

> God's grace is like a passing storm of rain which does not return where once it has been . . . it came to the Jews but passed over. Paul brought it to the Greeks but it passed over . . . the Romans and Latins had it. And you must not think that you have it forever.[13]

Church leaders therefore need to get a larger perspective. We must relinquish our obsession with counting, centralizing, trying to find ways of saving the Church. These are features of Babylon. In receiving we must recognize that God chooses what is weak to bring to nothing the things that are. Stop head-counting and panicking. Theological and spiritual discernment is required.

Being small and decentralized can enable Christians to concentrate much more on building new relationships. Without the distractions of building, structure and management Christians can give more time to prayer, worship, being hospitable, sharing the faith and reflecting theologically on their activities. Some churches may not remain small. Like the parable of the 'mustard seed' we should not set limits on the type of growth God may wish to bestow on us.

> The kingdom of God is like a mustard seed, which when sown into the ground, is the smallest of all the seeds on earth; yet when it is sown it grows up and becomes the greatest of all shrubs and puts forth large branches, so that the birds of the air can make nests in its shade. (Mk. 4.30f)

> In Mark's parables the seed is the Word. Growth in one form or another is given by God and inexplicable. Receiving comes after relinquishing.

The Survival of the Church in Babylon

1. Memory

> If I forget you, O Jerusalem, . . . let my tongue cling to the roof of my mouth, if I do not set Jerusalem above my highest joy. (Ps. 137.5)

The wisdom of the past is of little importance in Babylon. Driven by money and governed by technocrats and managers, memory is an immediate casualty. Its rapid erosion is an inevitable consequence of living in a fast moving society dependent on instant communication. Brueggemann comments 'When we have completely forgotten our past, we absolutize the present and we will be like contented cows in Bashan who want nothing more than the best of today'.[14] He describes memory as a magnet which draws the people of

God back to the past to give a new stimulus for 'prophetic imagination in the present'.[15]

Elijah returned to Horeb, the mountain of God. It was a place of theophany, earthquake wind and fire but God no longer spoke to him in that way. Instead Elijah had to retune his ears to hear God's new silent voice. Christian disciples living in Babylon should visit the holy places of old. The cathedrals have been mentioned already but there are other 'thin places' like Iona, Lindisfarne and the ancient ruins of Bolton Abbey and Glastonbury. There is also Ephesus and the letter to the Ephesians.

2. Citizenship

> You are no longer strangers and sojourners, but fellow citizens with the saints and members of the household of God. (Eph. 2.19)

Our Babylonian captivity has eroded the prophetic edge of church. Babylon's infiltration into its life has robbed churches of 'holiness'. There is however a subtle danger. If we attempt to relinquish the Babylon within we may end up exiling ourselves. Put bluntly we become a 'holy huddle'. Instead of being a 'saving community' we regard ourselves as a 'saved community' and live in our own isolated bubble.

If the pursuit of justice is to be a primary focus of mission then we dare not reduce the conversations

Exile?

we already have with the Babylon around us. To do so would be to disenfranchise ourselves and remove us further from politics. The word 'politics' comes from the Greek *polis:* a city. Ephesians tells us we are citizens both of the present world and of the world to come. We have a missionary task to 'make God's wisdom known to the principalities and powers (3.10). This is both spiritual and political. In Babylon the church has to become more political not less.[16]

The Jews during their long sojourn in exile experienced the State both in its oppressive and in its more benign form. Those second generation Jews who wished to return to Jerusalem were able to negotiate their release. Indeed in the time of Nehemiah they were able to find support from the State. In the Roman Babylon of the New Testament, Paul viewed the State in a less hostile way than the writers of 1 Peter and the book of Revelation. Today our conversations with Babylon will have elements both of confrontation and commendation depending on context, circumstance and the issue being addressed. Holiness in Babylon is political!

3. Doing theology

> Remember that you were at one time without Christ, being aliens and strangers. (Eph 2.12)

Survival in Babylon depends on reinterpreting Christianity's Biblical roots. Reflective theology

Exile?

becomes an essential tool for survival and renewal. You cannot restructure yourself out of Babylon! Psalm 137 poses the key theological question 'How can we sing the songs of Zion in a strange land.'

This first letter of Peter is addressed to exiles, strangers, temporary residents, and migrants (Pet. 1.1, 2.11). The writer takes Old Testament words and re-imagines them to create a theology of hope. Reflecting on Exodus 19.4–6 he tells the exiles that they are God's 'elect'. 'They are not punished with dispersion in a foreign land but 'chosen' for a task 'because of their honoured standing before God.'[17] He raids the book of Isaiah and pauses over the remarkable promise 'I am doing new things . . . I shall make a way in the wilderness . . . I give water so that my chosen people might drink, my people of whom I took possession for myself in order to recount my mighty acts' (Isa. 43.19–21). Peter seizes upon the image of a corner stone which people trip over (Isa. 8.4) before insisting that the stone is Christ 'chosen and honoured' (Isa. 28.16). Although rejected this stone becomes the head of the corner (Ps. 118.22). In re-imagining Scripture the writer is able to give God's people a 'living hope'.

He spells out their vocation. They are to be 'built into a spiritual house' and become a 'holy priesthood' (2.3) with an 'inheritance that is imperishable, undefiled, and unfading'. Christians in Babylon are holy because they have been set apart to reflect the suffering rejected Christ. Their theology is to be a theology of the cross. They are not living in darkness but dwell in his most marvellous light.

Behind these verses are echoes of Hosea. He spoke of God bringing Israel into the wilderness and making 'the Valley of Achor (trouble) a door of hope' (Hosea 2.15). Babylon may seem like a wilderness for some, but for others it is a place of discovery and renewal. God is making a future out of things that are not. He is choosing what is 'low and despised in this world, things that are not to reduce to nothing things that are' (1 Cor. 1.28).

Hope for the Church Babylon

Deep within most people, particularly in troubled times, is a longing to return to the past. Nostalgia springs from distant happy memories. But there can be no going back. An angel with a flaming sword bars the entrance gate of Eden. Hope is located in the future.

Diarmaid MacCulloch comments on how, since the Reformation, Western Christianity has often been polarized between those who embrace the Enlightenment and those who reject it.[18] As children of the Enlightenment we place our faith in reason. In thinking of the scientific and social advancement evident in our Western World we assume that human progress can continue. We already have the capacity to rid our planet of poverty, feed the hungry, reduce carbon emissions and save the planet, but will we do so?

The cross of Christ tells a different story. It exposes the darker side of human progress and shows that something lurks within each of us which cumulatively leads to the creation of Babylons. The death of Christ on the cross places a question mark against our optimism. It does not, however, put pessimism in its place. The vision of hope in the opening chapter of Ephesians rests not on human ingenuity but on the grace of God enacted in Christ and released by the Spirit in an extravagant flood of 'fullness' (Eph.1.23). Charles Taylor describes fullness in this way:

> Sometimes one experiences a fullness in which the world suddenly seems charged with meaning, coherence, and beauty that break in through our ordinary sense of being in the world.[19]

Whatever troubles assail us in Babylon and however bad things might get creation is still saturated with divine possibility and God will keep on leaking though into people's lives. The future will not be a reconstruction of the past. God will make a future out of things that are not because he chooses what is 'low and despised in this world to reduce to nothing the things that are' (1 Cor. 1.28).

I have already referred to the dynamic Trinity. Elsewhere I have described how when the Trinity turns towards the world, the Word and the Spirit

Exile?

become the two arms of God embracing all humanity. On the cross this dynamic partnership of Son, Spirit and Father is stretched to its ultimate limit to encompass and embrace the global pain of creation. In the resurrection the partners hug each other and all humanity is gathered up in that embrace. We live between the stretching and the gathering. For the Church in Babylon it is about relinquishing and receiving. We therefore find ourselves experiencing the spirituality of Easter Saturday. Behind are the shattered dreams of Calvary while a new Easter of faith lies before us.

NOTES

1. Jennifer Watkins (editor at Christian Solidarity worldwide), 'The Persecuted Church', *MET Connexion*, Autumn 2014.
2. James Laney, 'Our New Identity', in Logan, *Theology and Evangelism in the Wesleyan Heritage*, Nashville: Kingswood Books, 1994, p.178.
3. Walter Brueggemann, *Hopeful Imagination: Prophetic Voices in Exile*, Fortress Press, 1986, p.7.
4. Alasdair MacIntyre, *After Virtue: A Study in Moral Theory*, London: Duckworth, 1981, p.245.
5. Robert Schreiter, *Constructing Local Theologies*, London: SCM, 1985, pp.72f.
6. Simon Jenkins in his *Short History of England*, Profile Books, 2012, p.293. He was writing before the rise of popularism!

Exile?

7. Phil Potter, *Pioneering a New Future: A Guide to Shaping Change and Changing the Shape of the Church*, The Bible Reading Fellowship, 2015, p.170.
8. Potter, p.119.
9. Potter, p.121.
10. Jurgen Moltmann, *The Trinity and the Kingdom of God*, SCM Press, 1981.
11. Having struggled through Rowan Williams' reflections on the Trinity (*On Augustine*, Bloomsbury, 2016) I realize that it is not quite as simple as I am suggesting.
12. See Appendix 4:3. S. Bevans and R. Schroeder, *Constants in Context: A Theology of Mission for Today*, Orbis, 2004, p.7.
13. Gordon Rupp, *Principalities and Powers*, Wyvern Books, 1965, p.84.
14. Brueggemann, *Hopeful Imagination*, p.102.
15. Walter Brueggemann, *The Covenanted Self: Explorations in Law and Covenant*, Fortress Press, 1999, pp.23, 27.
16. Unfortunately the word 'politics' has become linked to 'party politics'. The politics I have in mind (and maybe the writer of Ephesians) is about citizenship and the creation of communities where the walls of division are being broken down.
17. D. Nienhuis and R. Wall, *Reading the Epistles of James, Peter, John and Jude*, Eerdmans, 2013,

p.114.
18. Diarmaid MacCulloch, *All things Made New: Writings on the Reformation*, Allen Lane, 2016, p.8.
19. A full discussion of fullness is to be found in Taylor's *Secular Age*, pp.1–22 and in the chapter 'Cross Pressures', pp.594–617.

8

METHODISM: WHERE WILL YOU BE?

Behold, I will open your graves, and raise you from your graves, O my people; and I will bring you home. (Ez. 11.12; Eph. 5.14–17)

I have spoken and written often about the Triune God, the fluidity of the Holy Spirit and the mysterious elective processes of God. I took up this theme in my address of 2005 (see Appendix) and again when I spoke to the Ministerial Session of Conference on 22nd June 2006.[1]

> We are standing on the edge of renewing waves of the Holy Spirit which we can either ride exuberantly into life, or be drowned into oblivion. There are two Greek words for 'time', *chronos* and *kairos*. The first word is clock-time measured by chronometers, the second relates to that moment when linear time and eternity are encapsulated in a single elective moment of opportunity. Unless an immediate response is made God's *kairos* moment passes. 'The time (*kairos*) is fulfilled and the kingdom of God is at hand; repent and believe in the gospel' (Mk. 1.14). Methodism is approaching a *'kairos* moment'; a brief window of opportunity, possibly only about

five years, in which to turn our church around, or to be more accurate 'to repent and believe'.[2]

Future Methodism

John Wesley modelled Methodism's mission from his reading of the Acts of the Apostles, where the first witnesses were ordinary people, fired by the Spirit to become 'extraordinary messengers'. Evangelism for him was a priority to be pursued regardless of formal church order. George Hunter sums up Wesley's understanding:

> The identity of the church is located in its apostolic mission and ministry to people (and to whole populations) who are not yet people of faith, and this ministry and mission are primarily entrusted to the laity.[3]

Wesley operated with two models of Church.[4] One was the historical institution served by professionals like himself which he found to be largely out of touch with the new industrial populations. His principal model was of a dynamic fellowship of believers who sought full salvation. Did he want his converts to become part of the Established Church as instruments of renewal? This did not happen. The two models failed to coalesce though there was some spill-over in the sympathetic evangelical parishes. Wesley's original organic movement, with the passage of time, turned

Methodism: Where Will You Be?

into a Church with its unique structures and ministry. Has Methodism now come full circle? Can we recover its early local dynamic? John Henry Newman was surely right to point out that 'if the Church is to remain the same, it must change'.

Methodism in Britain today has too many buildings; many in the wrong place. Our organization is cumbersome. I have lived with decline since my ministry began in 1965. We have attempted to stem the outgoing tide. Often forgetful of theology we have turned elsewhere for solutions and like King Hezekiah of old have inadvertently let Babylon (Isa. 39.1–6) take us into captivity.[5] So what of the future?

Church Growth theory propounds three necessary models of church corresponding to size: the cell (3–12 people), the congregation (25–175 people) and the celebration (175+ people).[6] Traditional mainline Protestant Churches have focused on the 'congregation', even when size has been below or above the numbers suggested. Should our Sunday morning congregational model, so beloved of traditional churches, now move to some other midweek time or location? I anticipate that the more effective model for the future may well be regular meetings of the cell with occasional large gatherings for celebration. I interpret 'cell' as anything from a midweek meeting in an old folks home, a house church or a 'fresh expression' of church as described in a previous chapter.[7] We

Methodism: Where Will You Be?

must not forget that cells can multiply and need not necessarily remain small (Mk. 4.30f).

Methodism needs to take on board the three key words from our last chapter: *smallness, decentralization and dispersion*. Given our Methodist story we should be able to respond to these three challenges. They were in our DNA from the beginning. Methodist 'societies' grew in number. Wesley's genius, unlike Whitefield's, was in creating a system which held dispersed communities together within a common framework of oversight. It has been suggested that we should see ourselves as a 'movement'. 'Movement', however, must not be seen as an alternative to 'church'.[9] I see 'movement' as a feature of a church which is a dynamic, fluid and flexible organism of the sort described in the Ephesian vision.

The Methodism of the future will inevitably be much smaller but, as John Vincent wisely reminds us, 'smallness is not a fatal flaw'. We must therefore rejoice in being modest.[8] Where-ever our churches (both 'inherited' and 'emerged') meet, the liturgy should relate directly to the daily life, struggles and experience of the worshippers. What is essential, however, is that the worship also draws its vitality and illumination from the universal treasures of Christian theology, tradition, hymnology and liturgy. The temptation in Babylon is to be pragmatic, ignore the riches of the past and offer DIY liturgies with a 'feel good' factor attractive

115

to 'outsiders'. In our consumer culture 'cheap grace' supported by a theology of glory and success instead of a theology of the cross may indeed increase numbers but may also produce new Gnostics.[10]

Methodism cannot compete with the cathedrals but we can still strive to create holy places through the use of imaginative symbols, music and testimony to evoke wonder and mystery. Here and also in our 'heritage sites', people hungry for spiritual reality can be fed. Above all the Eucharist will be celebrated in such a manner that the worshippers will be broken and blessed. A table set up in the wilderness brings healing to the world.

Methodism in Babylon

1. Dispersion and the kingdom of God

Our main focus in the future will be on the 'dispersed church' rather than the 'gathered church'. If we are to survive and thrive in Babylon we must repudiate our 'church-shaped-mission' and become a 'mission-shaped church'.

> Start with the Church and the mission will probably be lost. Start with mission and it is likely that the Church will be found.[11]

Already some 'emerging churches', not using Methodist premises, are giving us a foretaste of possible futures. How can we help these to multiply, become more diverse, more radical, more political and more 'kingdom' orientated?

Dudley Coates, one time Vice President of the Conference tells us that our intercessions reflect our priorities. If there is no big crisis happening in the wider world our prayers are mostly about ourselves and those who are ill. When prayers venture beyond the church walls they become 'anodyne and cover everything in general and not one thing in particular . . . how often do we hear prayers for accountants, lawyers, factory workers, civil servants . . . or those who work in betting shops?'[12] He says that Christians generally give out the vibes that they are not interested in what people do unless they work for the Church or are in the caring professions. He concludes:

> I believe that this attitude may well have made a significant contribution to the drop in church attendance . . . only if we learn from the world . . . have we any right to expect that people will want to hear the gospel.[13]

This is a prerequisite for living in Babylon. We have to listen and learn from the wider context if we are to redeem it.[14]

2. The Bible

The American scholar Albert Outler has produced what has been termed the 'Wesleyan Quadrilateral'. Wesley's successors are encouraged to do theology within a dynamic framework of four components; scripture, reason, tradition and experience. The quadrilateral is a functional tool kit subject to context. There is nothing sacred about it. The difficulty comes in trying to weigh and balance each of these components. In a yet to be published article I have argued that the Wesleyan quadrilateral is broken beyond repair.[15]

The rise of popularism, propaganda and image has dethroned reason. How is it to be restored?

Philip Jenkins has stated that the theology within the growing global church tends to be conservative.[16] Vibrant and conservative expressions of Christianity are not without their blind spots, as some worried liberal theologians from the traditional churches are all too ready to point out. It is not all sour grapes for what they rightly fear is the explosive cocktail of enthusiasm and fundamentalism. It has been said that 'a fundamentalist is simply an evangelical who is angry about something'. Fundamentalism is essentially a 'reactive' movement often against the modern world which is deemed to be a threat to its core values.[17]

Experience for Wesley was linked with the inner witness of the Holy Spirit. Today 'personal experience' has little to do with the Holy Spirit and everything to do with existential 'self-fulfilment'. As we shall see in our last chapter 'self-sacrifice' is not only deeply embedded in our tradition but is a counter cultural response to the self-assertive life of Babylon which is emptying our culture of grace.[18]

Tradition remains important and the 1932 Deed of Union is a firm reminder of our historic roots and providential purpose. Our Babylonian culture, however, creates amnesia and replaces tradition with pragmatic action and reaction. I conclude that Scripture within our Babylonian context must again become central.

> There is no basis in Wesley for treating reason, experience, or even Christian antiquity as authorities on an equal plane with Scripture. Scripture, while not being the sole *source* of all truth, was certainly taken to be the final *arbiter* of truth on all matters which Scripture addressed.[19]

In our Methodist theological supermarket we have been able to choose up to seven different ways of looking at the Bible. This approach has enabled us to span diversity but has it also had the unfortunate effect of emptying Scripture of its power and authority?[20]

3. The Spirit

The Gospel of John was probably written in Ephesus some twenty or thirty years after Paul was there. The church is having a hard time. Their most pressing challenge comes from what John calls the 'world' (*kosmos*). This word occurs many times in the Gospel but is mostly used to describe a hostile environment. Conflict rages between light and dark, truth and falsehood, death and life. Although God created the *kosmos* it is no longer friendly towards the disciples of Jesus. 'Principalities and powers' are at work, though John does not use these Pauline words. The writer of John reminds the disciples of the words of Jesus. 'If the world hates you, be aware that it hated me before it hated you. If you belonged to the world, the world would love you as its own' (John 15.18f).

The Holy Spirit in John has none of the effervescent characteristics of the book of Acts. Instead the Spirit is described as the 'comforter', the 'encourager,' the 'advocate'. The Spirit's role in adverse circumstance is to 'teach' and 'remind' (14.25). The Spirit is present to 'prove the world wrong' and to convict of 'sin, righteousness and judgement'. In our contemporary Babylon, the Holy Spirit is still at work but quietly and subtly; sustaining, enabling, judging, re-motivating and bringing to mind the words of Jesus.

Ministry in Babylon

Hunger and hurt are the starting points for ministers and congregations. Congregations will not care about the visions of the minister or leader until they know that the leader cares for them! Before the future can be contemplated, the past must be harnessed and honoured. Wounds may have to be healed. Potter suggests that we relinquish management models and look to the game of football.[21] Leaders lead not by imparting information but by communicating personal passion and inspiration. Dreams should be big, goals small. Achieving a modest target creates energy. A truly 'mission-shaped church' is made up of Christians who 'spin webs in the community'. The Church in Babylon instead of thinking of itself as a large symphony orchestra with a conductor should operate with invention and inspiration like a jazz band.

Most churches in the old paradigm model themselves on a swimming pool where people are invited to jump in. The future paradigm is more nerve racking. We are called to be 'surfers'.[22]

In terms of an overall pattern of ministry, John Finney gives Methodism a clue.[23] He contrasts the Roman and the Celtic styles of mission. The Roman method was to 'set up a skeleton organization and then evangelize. They structured for mission (as Methodism does today). The Celtic pattern was different. The Celtic bishops were not bureaucrats but evangelists who worked at the fringes (As Wesley did in his day). They gathered people together, initiated worship, and then created an appropriate framework for them. Worship was not in church buildings but centered on the high crosses dotted about the countryside. The Roman model was centralized (Babylon?) The Celtic model was localized and focused on dispersion. Methodism needs to relinquish the former and embrace the latter. Once the 'chairs of the district' were evangelists – but today?[24]

In 1965 Gordon Rupp, as President addressing the Ministerial Session of Conference, stated that Methodism was facing one of those 'turning points in the history of our church'.[25] He was addressing the decade when secularism was biting into our flesh. His subject was the 'pastoral office'. He argued that the 'vain prophecy' which was beguiling many ministers needed 'the corrective of history'. He suggested that the survival of God's people depended on the effectiveness of the pastor.

> The thought of Christ as Shepherd is not marginal to the New Testament view of ministry but it goes pretty near the heart of the matter.

In speaking of how the good shepherd lays down his life for the sheep he said, 'without caring to the point of sacrifice . . . all our training and our equipment, old or new, become gadgets and gimmicks . . . We must think of people rather than geography'. The most moving part of his address were his reflections on the obituaries of four ministers; one who died in 1777, one in 1802, one in 1873 and the fourth in 1953. He invoked these to show that although contexts and patterns change, exercising the ministry of Christ the Shepherd gave these ministers in their vocation of sacrificial service a spirit of joy, fulfilment and radiance.

John Wesley produced his hymn book in 1779. Some years later a Supplement was added. It has an intriguing section entitled 'The Ministry and Prayers for Ministers'. I conclude this chapter with a verse of one of these hymns:

> Gracious Spirit, dwell with me!
> I myself would gracious be,
> And with words that help and heal
> Would thy life in mine reveal;
> And with actions bold and meek
> Would for Christ my Saviour speak.

NOTES

1. This is a quote from my Presidential Address to the Ministerial Session of Conference in 2006. I first wrote of this dynamic in *Into the Far Country: A Theology of Mission for an Age of Violence*, Epworth Press, 2003. The same message has also appeared (briefly) in my next two books, *Beyond the Box*, 2006 and *On the Edge of Pentecost*, 2007.
2. Although some bold experiments have taken place in the past ten years regrettably Methodism as a whole has been too slow in responding to the *kairos* moment.
3. George Hunter III, *To Spread the Power: Church Growth in the Wesleyan Spirit*, Nashville: Abingdon

Press, p.159.
4. Howard A. Snyder, *The Radical Wesley and Patterns of Church Renewal*, Illinois: InterVarsity Press, 1980, p.71.
5. Over and against decline here is Methodism's story of growth elsewhere. It is has been estimated that the membership of the Methodist family beyond Europe and the US is increasing at a rate of about 1 million new members per year.
6. Roy Pointer, *How Do Churches Grow?* Basingstoke: Marshalls Paperbacks, 1984, p.51.
7. Once a month for the past seven years I celebrate communion with a small group of elderly Methodist ladies (most in their 80s and 90s). Their local Methodist church was closed and they now meet in the back room of a Baptist Church. The number hovers around 8 to 10. They are wonderful! Even though death or illness reduces the numbers, there are new people coming.
8. John Vincent, *Methodism Unbound: Christ and Methodism for the 21st Century*, Church in the Market Place Publications, 2015, p.82.
9. John Vincent says 'Methodism is not a Movement all the time, but encourages its members and minister to be it' (ibid., 96) While I do not disagree with this, my perspective arises from the theology of Ephesians and the dynamic of the ebb and flow of the Holy Spirit.
10. Gnosticism is an early Christian heresy made up of diverse sets of beliefs giving an individual a secret

knowledge of God. In its modern form you will find it in highly spiritual individuals who always seem to have a direct hot-line to God. 'God told me to say this to that person', 'When I pray I always get a parking space'. It is a theology of glory. It almost always leads to self-deception and an inflated ego which can harm others.

11. *Mission-Shaped Church*, Church of England Publishing, 2004, p.124.
12. Dudley Coates, *Shades of Grey: Making Choices in Uncertainty*, Inspire, 2006, p.5.
13. Ibid., pp.126f.
14. While I have used the word 'Babylon', Justin Welby uses the word 'mammon'. I think we are both describing the same thing. To dethrone mammon two things are required. 'We dethrone by listening. Then we enthrone Christ by listening and acting.' (*Dethroning Mammon: Making Money Serve Grace*, Bloomsbury, 2016, p.148.)
15. This document can be found on my web site, www.tomstuckey.me.uk
16. Philip Jenkins, *The Next Christendom: The Coming of Global Christianity*, Oxford: Oxford University Press, 2002, p.194.
17. Alister McGrath, *The Future of Christianity*, Oxford: Blackwell Publishers, 2002, pp.74f. This may be particularly so with Islamic fundamentalists.
18. Miroslav Volf, *Free of Charge: Giving and Forgiving in a Culture Stripped of Grace*, Zondervan, 2005.
19. Ben Witherington III, 'The Theological Roots of

Wesley's View of Evangelism', found in James Logan (ed.), *Theology and Evangelism in the Wesleyan Heritage*, Kingswood Books, 1994, p.64.

20. Donald English argued that the Bible was the 'centre piece for our knowledge of God through Jesus by the Holy Spirit'. He saw reason, tradition and experience revolving around the Bible like the dangling pieces of a baby's mobile.

21. Phil Potter, *Pioneering a New Future: A Guide to Shaping Change and Changing the Shape of the Church*, The Bible Reading Fellowship 2015, pp.119f.

22. Ibid., pp.172f.

23. John Finney, *Recovering the Past*, London: DLT, 1996, p.86.

24. 'Chairs of the District', possibly to be called 'District Superintendents' (some see them as the equivalent to Anglican Bishops), originally acted as district evangelists.

25. Gordon Rupp, 'No Ministry in isolation from the Church', *Methodist Recorder*, 3rd July 1969.

9

WAKE UP, METHODISM!

Everything exposed by the light becomes visible, for everything that becomes visible is light. Therefore it says, 'Sleeper, awake! Rise from the dead, and Christ will shine on you.'

Be careful then how you live, not as unwise people but as wise, making the most of the time, because the days are evil. So do not be foolish, but understand what the will of the Lord is. (Eph. 5.14–17)

On Sunday, 4th April 1742, Charles Wesley preached before the University of Oxford on the text 'Awake, Thou That Sleepest'. According to one witness it was not well received. Charles was 'hissed out of the pulpit'.[1]

When I addressed the Ministerial Session of Conference on 22nd June 2006, I spoke of repentance and insisted that Methodism must act quickly. We have not! Babylon has further infiltrated our systems. Moreover the world's political and economic situation has become more precarious. We need to wake up!

Wesley's sermon was delivered in troubled times. It was an urgent and passionate message! England

Wake Up, Methodism!

was engaged in a war against Spain. Things were not going well. Walpole's long standing government had collapsed. The Young Pretender was preparing his plans to regain the English throne. Wesley exclaims:

> It is time for us to awake from our sleep before the 'great trumpet of the Lord be blown' and our land become a field of blood. O may we speedily see the things that make for peace, before they are hid from our eyes!

Strong stuff! It makes our contemporary Methodist 'wake up' calls sound timid. Richard Jackson, looked at the reports of the 2016 Conference and declared:

> London, we have a problem . . . I looked in vain for anything that might have indicated hints of a radical departure from what we have been doing traditionally in Methodism throughout so many years of decline. There were few indications of an emergency being acknowledged . . . we are reduced to about 200,000 members and our age profile is that of a Saga cruise ship.[2]

Alastair Bolt in another *Recorder* article rebukes Methodism for avoiding the real problem:

> Over the years many good people have done many good things. There have been serious if often belated attempts to solve problems and come up with new ideas, but the metaphysic has

not been addressed. Everything has laboured around a profound void in personal and corporate experience of a supernatural, tangible and accessible God.[3]

He concludes that all our efforts are of no avail because we have not sufficiently addressed the issue of divine encounter in worship.

'Know your disease! Know your cure!' was the dictum John Wesley employed.[4] His diagnosis of humanity's problem was that the image of God within had become distorted. Although reason and practical activity were important for him he believed that only the transcendent power of God's grace could work the cure.

Repentance

1. Our systems

Repentance is not only about reducing our heavy Connexional System, which for some is a source of 'structural stressing' and for many at grass-roots an irrelevancy; repentance requires a spiritual change of heart. Our church needs the Spirit 'not so much as the oil of charism but more like WD40 – freeing up rather than blessing up'.[5] Charles asks 'Dost thou love the Lord thy God will all thy heart, and with all thy mind, and with all thy soul, and with all thy strength'? Addressing the externals of faith he states that circumcision and uncircum-

Wake Up, Methodism!

cision 'availeth nothing unless God puts his Spirit within you, and causes you to walk in my statutes'. Relinquishing is an essential requirement for the churches in Babylon and even more so for us. With reference to Ezekiel 37 Charles contemplates the valley of dry bones and exclaims:

> Thou poor unawakened sinner . . . O that as I prophecy, there might now be 'a noise and a shaking'.

2. Our worship

I have suggested that we have reversed the great commandment. Our failure to love God with all our heart, mind and soul is revealed in our worship. 'God is dangerous'. I used this sentence in my Presidential address.[6] Out of the dozen five-minute local radio interviews on the following day, seven interviewers latched on to this phrase. I responded by saying that in so much of our worship God had been reduced and tamed. He has become a pale substitute for the 'Bible God' who shakes kingdoms and revolutionizes lives. The American writer Annie Dillard brilliantly expresses what I sometimes feel.

> Why do people in church seem like cheerful brainless tourists on a package tour of the Absolute? Does anyone have the foggiest idea of what sort of power we blithely invoke? Congregations are like children playing on the floor with their chemistry sets, mixing up a batch

of TNT to kill off the boredom of Sunday morning. It is madness for ladies to wear straw hats to church; we should all be wearing crash helmets. Stewards should issue life preservers and signal flares; they should lash us to our pews.[7]

Early Methodists believed in the evangelical power of the Word. Kenneth Cracknell says, 'Wesley knew in his bones that only by being preached would the Word of God reveal its fullest meaning.'[8] While Methodism has given some attention to the content and format of worship we have not sufficiently explored how we can prayerfully develop faith with an expectation of divine intervention.

We must repent of putting God in a box and of being content with worship that is interesting rather than inspiring. Charles addresses those who say 'we do not deny the *assistance* of God's Spirit; but only this *inspiration*, this *receiving* the Holy Spirit and being *sensible* of it. Against such reductionism he declares:

> Pray that we may be filled with the Holy Spirit . . . Therefore, to deny any of these, is to renounce the Church of England, as well as the whole Christian revelation.

When worship loses its potency; mission loses its efficacy.

3. Our pastoral care

Wake Up, Methodism!

Pastoral ministry is relational and 'face-to-face' personal. As Gordon Rupp pointed out, the office of 'shepherd' is central to the presbyter's vocation. The 'good shepherd' knows his sheep and lays down his life for them (Jn. 10.14). Sadly and tragically, the culture of Babylon is driving this from the heart of some ministers so that they no longer have the time or the energy for giving spiritual care and direction.[9]

In my previous chapter, I used the word 'decentralize'. Does this imply further structural reorganization, or do we already have the framework within our system? How can Methodism stop devising new tasks to burden already busy superintendents? Surely an essential task of the ordained in a busy world is to keep people from being busy?

Unfortunately the legacy of John Wesley's *Rules for a Helper* encourages us to fill our diaries.[10] The pace of life was much slower for Wesley and it had a natural rhythm to it. He spent many hours on horse-back thinking, reading, praying, observing, singing and sharing conversation with his travelling companions.[11] Charles, unlike his brother, did not in later life travel the length and breadth of the land yet for both brothers pastoral care was paramount. Have we allowed other things to swamp our pastoral vocation? If so we must repent.

Charles in his sermon reflects on Peter, lying in a dark dungeon bound with two chains.[12] Babylon is our contemporary prison. For some it is a comfortable prison yet it is still a place of subtle captivity. Charles exclaims. 'O may the Angel of the Lord come upon thee, and make the light shine into thy prison!'

Words, silence and sacrifice

Our fatal flaw is our inability to talk to others about God. We do exercise a powerful witness through our serving and caring so why do we not speak of it or of the Jesus who inspires it? English reticence? Lack of confidence? Not knowing what to say? What irony! Our world is awash with words, tweets, and messaging; yet we remain tongue-tied. We have no difficulty in talking to others about our hobbies, our families, our holidays and maybe even church, but does God get a mention?

At root we do not speak of God because there is no passion for God in our hearts. We do not love God with all our heart, our soul and our mind. The components here are testimony, integrity and theology.

Can we be trained to 'talk about God'? Study programmes exist and if not suitable for Methodists we can surely create our own, but is this enough? I maintain that unless our words come out of the Divine Silence within, they will lack depth and efficacy. This inner silence is born of solitude. It is a by-product of self-denial, suffering and sacrificial love. It is the silence behind the words that touches people's hearts.[13] In his letter to the Corinthians, Paul lines up the learned teachers, the literary experts, the clever consultants, the brilliant debaters with the express purpose of exposing the emptiness of their utterances. Without this inner witness we are but 'clashing cymbals and booming gongs' (1 Cor. 13). Henri Nouwen says:

> Solitude, silence, and prayer allow us to save ourselves and others from the shipwreck of our self-destructive society. The temptation is to go mad with those who are mad.[14]

Nouwen's phrase 'save ourselves' is unfortunate; or is it? The early sermons of the Wesleys kept echoing the New Testament question 'what must I do to be saved?' Babylon also offers personal salvation.

> You can save yourself through 'self-assertion' and then move on to 'self-fulfilment'. Happiness can be achieved through the pursuit of money and through the sacrament of shopping.

The counter-cultural message of Methodism is 'you can find salvation by faith in Christ and happiness and holiness through the way of obedience and self-sacrifice'. The word 'sacrifice' is an unacceptable word in Babylon.[15] Over the past fifty years of ministry I have tried to affirm this ethic of 'self-sacrifice' through the words of the annual Covenant Service.

> Put me to doing, put me to suffering, let me be employed for you or laid aside for you, exalted for you or brought low for you.

Sadly I have come to see that in fulfilling this vocation, my family members have also borne something of the 'down-side' of my sacrifice. Over and against this, however, I observe that everyone in Babylon sacrifices everyone else in their pursuit of money and self-fulfilment. Over and against this I reflect that as a presbyter the Church has gifted me with the security of money, a job, a house and the ability to choose how I spend my time. Such gifts are luxurious compared to the life-style which many around me are forced to adopt.

Taking up the cross is self-denial and sacrifice. It is about costly grace. In the Covenant Service we now have the option of using a different set of words more in tune with our culture. 'Your will be done when I am valued and when I am disregarded; when I find fulfilment and when it is lacking.' I cannot fault the theology yet I am left wondering if it is still about 'costly grace' when I remember that the majority of Christians in the world today are suffering persecution of one sort or another. I therefore come back to Charles Wesley and sing:

> Ready for all Thy perfect will,
> My acts of faith and love repeat,

Wake Up, Methodism!

Till death thy endless mercies seal,
And make the sacrifice complete.[16]

Praying and living the Ephesian vision

Charles, in the third point of his sermon, focuses on God's promise:

> How encouraging a consideration is this, that whosoever thou art, who obeyest His call, thou canst not seek His face in vain! If thou even now 'awakest, and arisest from the dead', He hath bound Himself to 'give thee light'.

Ephesians is soaked in prayer. The first chapter is a glorious expression of adoration and thanksgiving where the writer, after having blessed and praised God, prays for revelation (1.18). After three chapters of contemplating the 'riches of our glorious inheritance' we come to a prayer for illumination and inspiration (3.14–20). With the light comes the injunction to be 'filled with the Spirit'. The counter-cultural ethics and actions of chapters 4, 5 and 6 then hurl us into a confrontation with Babylon and the necessity for prayers of petition and intercession. There are two types of prayer here (6.18–20). 'All-prayer' is the spirituality of living a life constantly tuned into God's presence while 'supplications' are the more specific petitions triggered by this life in the Spirit.[17]

The writer of Ephesians suggests that God will keep leaking into people's lives as surprise 'flashes from beyond'. Everyone gets them but we Christians 'with the eyes of our heart enlightened' recognize them as divine epiphanies. My wife calls them 'God moments'. A gentleman in one of her meetings shared the following:

> The Christmas Eve midnight communion had just finished. As I was leaving the church I was surprised to hear a robin singing. You silly thing! What are you doing up at midnight? Then I looked at all the Christmas lights illuminating the area and realized that the bird thought it was daytime. The robin was celebrating the light that had come into the world.

Even in the brassiness of Babylon such 'Wow' moments still happen. David, a friend of mine, calls them 'Ah' moments and recounts his experience.

> I was present at a concert when Barry Manilow's hit song 'One Voice' was sung. There were many thousands in the audience. Many had candles and these were lit from each other. Gradually a flood of light rippled through the arena as individuals caught the fire and became one light and one voice. For me, and for many others, it was an 'Ah' moment. The experience 'moved beyond a purely emotional moment'. I thought of

'Jesus as the light of the world memory'.[18]

There is a wonderful rhythm in the Ephesian letter. Worship, praise and thanksgiving flow out into the world through mission and ministry. The letter ends with a prayer for Paul to have the 'boldness to speak'. Then comes the final declarations of peace, grace and love which propel us back to chapter one again. The letter goes round in a big circle.

For future Methodists it suggests that there should be a dynamic interplay between the small worshipping group committed to social holiness through action and reflection; and the larger worshipping and celebrating congregation. The worship in the larger congregation needs to evoke deep memory through inspiring Biblical preaching with worship fed by the rich liturgical traditions of the past. There is a rhythm in worship and mission as they circle around the large and the small, the present and the past.

'Sit, walk, stand' was the dynamic suggested at the end of chapter two. Prayer again binds these together in Ephesians. Although the letter begins with worship and the looking up to God it ends with mission and the looking out to the world.

The chapel of the Episcopal Seminary of the South-West at Austin, Texas, is imaginatively designed to link church and world, worship and service. A former lecturer in liturgical studies, Dr L.

Brown, made much of the need for a balance between worship and engaged living. He sought to build up a healthy rhythm in Christian life style. The modern chapel has a light interior with plain glass windows behind the communion table through which the worshippers can see a large cross in the open air on the lawn beyond. The congregation is never allowed to feel closed off but made aware of the call for sacrificial living in the world beyond the chapel where Jesus waits to meet us.[19]

The future of Methodism

Our future does not depend on upgrading premises, tinkering with structures, devising new strategies either local or connexional. We will have a future when prayer rather than projects saturate our agenda. We will have a future when presbyters drag themselves away from their computers and get out and talk to people, helping them to pray, discover God in the world and talk about it. We will have a future when Methodists, who long to love God with all their heart, mind and soul, feel the encouragement of each other and know the transforming power of the Spirit. This is not rocket science. Charles, in his sermon, links his 'wake up' call with a demand for repentance and return.

His judgements are abroad in the earth; and we

Wake Up, Methodism!

have reason to expect the heaviest of all even that He should come unto us quickly, and remove our candlestick out of its place, except we repent and do the first works, unless we return to the principles of the Reformation, the truth and simplicity of the gospel.

Methodists are called to live in God's Easter Saturday. We are not called to save the church but to seek the kingdom of God. We are called to a life of self-sacrifice because that is the only way to self-fulfilment. We are called to live with a theology of the cross rather that a theology of glory.

My Presidential address began with Ezekiel's vision in chapter 37 and posed the question 'Can these bones live?' Ezekiel's message is about divine absence and return.[20] The message of Ezekiel (and Revelation) is that temples disappear but rivers of living water still bubble up. Charles reminds us that Methodism still has an unfinished task.

> When first sent forth to minister the word,
> Say, did we preach ourselves, or Christ the Lord?
> Was it our aim disciples to collect,
> To raise a party, or found a sect?
> No, but to spread the power of Jesus' name,
> Repair the walls of our Jerusalem
> Revive the piety of ancient days,
> And fill the earth with our Redeemer's praise.[21]

NOTES

1. Edward Sugden (ed.) *Wesley's Standard Sermons*, Volume 1, London: Epworth Press, 1966, pp.68f.
2. *The Times* of 30th August 2014 (slightly changed).
3. 'The Root of the Problem', *Methodist Recorder*, 10th March 2017.
4. Theodore Runyon, *The New Creation: Wesley's Theology Today*, Nashville: Abingdon Press, 1998, p.22.
5. Martyn Atkins, *Resourcing Renewal: Shaping Churches for the Emerging Future*, Inspire, 2007, p.59.
6. Appendix 2:4.
7. Annie Dillard, *Teaching a Stone to Talk: Expeditions and Encounters*, London: HarperPerennial, 1984, pp.40f. I have changed it slightly.
8. Kenneth Cracknell, *Our Doctrines: Methodist Theology as Classical Christianity*, Cliff College Publishing, 1998, p.82.
9. Why is it that some ministers do not 'work a room' building new relationships? Why is it that with the hundreds of people using our premises some ministers do not have the time to be around for the toddler's groups or slimming club? Is it shyness? Can one exercise ministry without establishing relationships of trust?
10. The first Rule for a Helper was: 'Be diligent. Never be unemployed for a moment. Never be triflingly employed. Never while away time; neither spend

any more time at any place than is strictly necessary.' Was this ethic a critique of the indulgent and lazy life style of some of the Anglican clergy of his time?

11. He was by all accounts a cheerful traveller who made the best of every situation (John Waller, *John Wesley: A Personal Portrait*, SPCK, 2003, p.92).
12. Charles turns this story into song, H&P, 216.
13. There is a marked difference in Peter's testi-mony on the two sides of Pentecost; denial before, powerful affirmation after. What caused the transformation? Brokenness and repent-ance. After he had embraced the 'Calvary Road' he no longer uttered empty words but spoke with a tongue of fire. Roy Hession wrote a little book with this title graphically describing the path we must take to renewal. 'At the foot of the Cross is a low door, so low that to get through it one has to stoop and crawl through. It is the only entrance to the Highway. We must go through it if we would go farther on our way. This door is called the Door of the Broken Ones' (The Calvary Road, Christian Literature Crusade London, 1950, p.26).
14. Henri Nouwen, *The Way of the Heart: Desert Spirituality and Contemporary Ministry*, DLT, 1981, p.92.
15. See footnote 5, Chapter 4.
16. Hymn, H&P, 745.
17. Andrew Lincoln, *Ephesians: Word Biblical Commentary*, Nashville: Nelson, 1990,

p.452.
18. I am indebted to Rev David Coote for this story.
19. I am indebted to Rev John Walker for this illustration.
20. Joseph Blenkinsopp, *Ezekiel, Interpretation. A Biblical Commentary for Teaching and Preaching*, John Knox, 1990, p.5.
21. Quoted in the front piece of George Hunter III, To Spread the Power: Church Growth in the *Wesleyan Spirit*, Nashville: Abingdon Press, 1987.

APPENDIX

10

DRY BONES

So I prophesied as I was commanded.
(Ezekiel 37.7)

1:1 There is a remarkable passage in Ezekiel 37 describing Israel as a valley of dry bones. Is God saying to Methodism 'can these bones live?' Some churches appear to have a death wish in their resistance to change. 'Over my dead body' is the slogan. Ezekiel's response to God's question is, 'O Lord God, you know'. God replies, 'Prophecy to these bones, and say to them: O dry bones, hear the word of the Lord . . . I will lay sinews on you and will cause flesh to come upon you . . . and put breath in you, and you shall live; and you shall know that I am the Lord.' The prophet obeys. There is a lot of rattling, clattering and reconnecting. Note the three stages: the first is about the skeleton or structure, the bringing together of bone to bone.

1:2 Methodism has been doing this for years as we keep restructuring ourselves. Although structures and plans can enable they do not give life. Only the Word of God and the Holy Spirit can energize. Have we recently experienced the breath of God and the power of the Holy Spirit? 'O Lord God you know.'

Dry Bones

1:3 The Spirit is rattling our bones! What is the Spirit saying? God is telling us that he has not yet finished with Methodism but is rather preparing us for a new future. He is calling us to radical change. He is speaking to us about repentance and conversion! God is telling us to create 'fresh expressions of church' alongside the old since much of the old, in its resistance to change, will not survive. Life comes to our dry bones only through prophesy, that is speaking the Word of the Lord and by the power of the Holy Spirit.

1:4 The report 'Time to talk of God' tells us that although we are good at conversations and socializing 'we are much less comfortable with seeking out or providing opportunities for conversation that allow us to go really deep, and to get real with each other about our faith'. This is because of our neglect of theology. I am puzzled how often, when I preach, after the service someone will say 'you made us think today'. Does this mean that the congregation is not normally given much to think about? Does it mean that they didn't understand a word of what I said? I get worried when I hear a minister or local preacher say 'of course I am not a theologian'. What has happened to theology – to thinking and speaking about God? The very word 'theology' is made up of two words: *theos* – God, and *logos* – word. With no theology the bones will not live!

1:5 The first of my two Presidential priorities is to focus on theology. I want to encourage us to develop confidence in evangelism and in our ability to speak of God in a meaningful way. Secondly I wish to focus on the Holy Spirit as we seek to develop fresh ways of being church. In the Youth Conference Report you will find the following sentence. 'Youth Conference recognized a lack of presence of the Holy Spirit within our weekly services and the need for the power and presence of the Holy Spirit to be more widely understood and appreciated.'

1:6 Word and Spirit need each other. When the Word is without the Spirit the Church dries up. When the Spirit is without the Word the Church blows up. When Word and Spirit come together the Church grows up. If we are to re-capture vision we must give attention to theology and the work of the Holy Spirit. Let's do some theology now on the Holy Spirit.

What sort of God?

2:1 In its doctrine of the Trinity, the Western Church emphasizes the one God who is revealed in three subsisting persons. A local preacher, who is to be congratulated for preaching on Trinity Sunday, told me how he explained the Trinity. He said 'I am father to my children, son to my parents and husband to my wife'. I suspect that most of us view the Trinity in this way and place emphasis on the one of God – a single person rather than three persons in partnership and communion. Concentrating on oneness creates a static Church, keen to organize, centralize and control. Diversity and creativity is swallowed up in the drive for unity.

2:2 The early Greek theologians of the Eastern Church emphasized the distinctiveness of the persons of the Trinity. They used the word *perichoresis*, which literally means 'to proceed about each other' to describe movement within the Trinity. There is a sort of barn dance; a flow and flux going on within God; a finding and a losing, a circling and spiralling of partners until all three are transfigured in each other, lost in a love-making out of which new universes are conceived and born. When the Trinity turns towards the world, the Word and the Spirit become the two arms of God embracing all humanity. On the cross this dynamic partnership of Son, Spirit and Father is stretched to its ultimate limit to encompass and embrace the global pain within creation. In the resurrection the partners hug each other and us in the joy of a world redeemed. So the Trinity, to change the imagery, is like a vast cosmic sea of love ebbing and flowing; ever changing yet ever the same.

2:3 There is a story about St Augustine. He was walking up and down on the sea shore at Carthage, puzzling over the Trinity. He had written hundreds of chapters on the subject across fifteen books and was no closer to unravelling the mystery. This theological bishop saw a little boy running backwards and forwards with a pot, filling it with sea-water and then running back to pour it into a hole he had dug in the sand. He kept repeating the exercise in an attempt to fill the hole. St Augustine watched him for some time. Finally he went over to the lad and said 'what are you doing?' 'I am trying to get that', said the lad pointing to the sea, 'into that', pointing to the hole. Augustine then realized why he was having trouble describing the Trinity.

2:4 We Methodists in our neglect of theology have dumbed down the message and domesticated God. We have lost the mystery. In our talk of a God of love we have forgotten, that like the raging sea, God is dangerous. We have not only put God in a box but we have become so used to transporting God around in buckets that God has ceased to be God. We have tamed the terror. We have managed the mystery. One thing is required, 'we must repent!'

What sort of mission?

3:1 Christ the 'Word' is active toward creation while the 'Spirit' of the Triune God is active in creation. The Holy Spirit is God 'turned inside out' in the world. Theologians are not confined to those who write incomprehensible books. Composers, sculptors, painters, artists are also theologians. Maybe theology is better served by creative artists than by ecclesiastical scholars? I regard Michelangelo as a theologian exploring the boundaries between the physical and the spiritual. His statue of Moses radiates power; spirit breaking out of stone. This is what we are meant to be yet so often we are like his 'prisoners'; unfinished statues of figures struggling to free themselves from the grip of marble.

3:2 Today the Holy Spirit, in a New Pentecost, is blowing across the world creating new Christians amongst the poor in the Southern continents. In the rich West, that very same Spirit is also surfacing, but in the longings of people outside the Church.

3:3 Jesus, in John 3, speaks of the Spirit blowing like the wind. His conversation with Nicodemus quickly fizzles out. Not so with the woman at the well in chapter 4. She is the better theologian and relentlessly presses Jesus to explain. She is the outsider who desperately wants living water to bubble up in her life. I am persuaded that it is in our encounters with people outside the Church that we will more frequently encounter the 'I am' of God. Inderjit Bhogal when he was Methodist President told us this story:

3:4 Graham was homeless and lives on the streets of Sheffield. People regarded him as a tramp, but Inderjit knew him. On one occasion they got into a conversation.

'I'm working on a sermon about tables, bread and parties in the wilderness', says Inderjit.

'I love bread.' said Graham.

He then broke off a large piece and gave it to Inderjit who took it, said 'Amen' and slowly ate it. Inderjit comments: 'all around us in this city environment there were people with a lifestyle of grabbing, greed and profit. People racing about yet here I was being fed by one of the poorest people I know. I was his honoured guest at a table in the wilderness.'

3:5 The Holy Spirit is surfacing especially in our encounters with the poor and the marginalized. It is often here that Word and Spirit come together in a moment of 'fullness' to turn a common place into a holy space.

What about the Church?

4:1 He came home from the church meeting exasperated and said to his wife 'I don't think I will go again'. Andrew has a highly responsible job. Arriving home from work at 7.30 pm he spent a few minutes with his young son before rushing out to the Church Council. There had been little time to

Dry Bones

talk or eat. The church meeting finished at 10.45 pm. The minister had no idea how to chair it and they spent nearly an hour talking about the flower rota. Andrew had so much to give but vowed he would never go again because they were only interested in talking trivialities. Like many of our young people he has abandoned the church.[1]

4:2 This story tells us that the institutional Church is in big trouble. While the world rushes by like a river in flood, nice people spend hours debating whether to take out a few pews. It is hardly surprising that disillusioned members drop out. John Wesley said, 'I am not afraid that the people called Methodists should ever cease to exist, but I am afraid lest they should only exist as a dead sect, having the form of religion without the power.' Is his fear now being realized? Are we trying to preserve telephone kiosks in the age of the mobile phone? The Spirit is seeking to make the Church into the vibrant vehicle of God's tomorrow not the museum piece of God's yesterday. In the report *What is a Circuit Superintendent?* you will find these words:

> Methodism arose as a missionary movement. Wesley's focus was upon the Spirit of God burning like a fire in the hearts of converted individuals, renewing the Church, firing communities and spreading until scriptural holiness covers the whole earth. His vision was of

the restoration and renewal of all things through grace.

That's the vision. We have a structure. We now need the Spirit and the Word.

4:3 Bevans and Schroeder in their huge book on mission published last year begin with the sentence, 'One of the most important things Christians need to know about the church is that the church is not of ultimate importance'.[2] This is a stunning sentence for two Roman Catholic theologians. What is ultimate for them is mission. 'Mission is seeing what God is doing in the world and joining in.' We in the West have substituted 'church' for 'Spirit' as the third person of the Trinity and in so doing have reversed God's understanding of mission. God has a mission; we are invited through the Holy Spirit to participate in it. When the Church does not join with what God is doing in the world then Church ceases to be Church and becomes a club. What some view as the decline of the Church institution is simply God passing judgement on nostalgic religious clubs.

4:4 If I had my way I would do two things. First, I would make sure that in every circuit there was at least one member of staff, presbyter, deacon or lay-worker, who having the gift of an evangelist, was released from pastoral charge and given responsibility for generating a 'new form of church' either through chaplaincy or through work with young people. (*This was greeted with a cheer!*)

4:5 Second, in order to release money and staff for this purpose I would shift power from the local church to the circuit meeting and make it the primary unit of mission. Given extra legal authority, the circuit meeting would then be able to close resistant churches, sell off the buildings and use the proceeds to employ and deploy staff in imaginative ways. (*This was greeted with a further cheer and general applause.*)

What sort of struggle?

5:1 As the Holy Spirit passes judgement upon the Church and pushes us in new directions we can feel a bit like Corporal Jones in *Dad's Army* who stamps about in circles bleating, 'Don't panic, don't panic.' God is punching holes in the institution because he wants to reshape it. We must reclaim our heritage as Methodists and remind ourselves that we were once a missionary movement of the Spirit with a particular concern for the marginalized.

5:2 It is hard for ministers and church leaders to maintain a passion for God in a declining Church. There comes a time when one's energy runs out. This happened to me in my second appointment. It was the era of the 'radical Christianity' of Harvey

Dry Bones

Cox and the first bubbling of the 'charismatic movement'. In my spiritual need I sought God. A Roman Catholic priest helped me. From beyond Methodism I have since learnt of the significance of silence, of contemplation, of dialogue and the importance of inculturation in our missionary enterprise. Without Spirit we dry up. Without Word and reflective theology we blow up. What holds both together is not our strength, but our vulnerability, for we have this treasure in earthen vessels.

5:3 So I return to Ezekiel 37, and the valley of dry bones. I do so because some of us, in our struggles to follow Christ, still carry hurts and are ever aware of our own frailties and failures. Some of us know inner pain too deep for words. There has been and there is a wilderness within; a valley of dry bones. Yet this place of brokenness is the renewing and restoring place of Spirit and Word.

> Ring the bells that still can ring
> Forget your perfect offering.
> There is a crack in everything,
> That is how the light gets in.[3]

[A video of waves beating on the shore began at this point as I continued to speak.]

5:4 The waves of Spirit are beating on the shore. God is calling us to launch out into the deep until our feet no longer touch the bottom. Methodism is not finished. It stands on the threshold of a new discovery of itself. Come Holy Spirit. Disturb our complacency. Drive away our fears. Remind us of the faith we have forgotten. Breathe your fluid life into us until the living waters of Spirit well up, washing, cleansing and renewing. Then carry us on the tides of your love into the very mystery of your being.

> Spirit of the Living God,
> Fall afresh on me.
> Spirit of the living God,
> Fall afresh on me,
> Break me, melt me,
> Mould me, fill me.
> Spirit of the living God,
> Fall afresh on me.[4]

Above is the full script of my address to the Representative Session of Conference. I have slightly shortened it. You can still LISTEN to it on: www.tomstuckey.me.uk

NOTES

1. Tom Stuckey. *Beyond the Box*, Inspire 2005, p.1.
2. Bevans and Schroeder, *Constants in Context: Theology of Mission Today*, Orbis Books, 2004.
3. Leonard Cohen, 'Anthem'.

Dry Bones

4. H&P, 295. This was sung quietly by a single voice but gradually more and more people spontaneously joined in as it was repeated again and again until all present were voicing a prayer of hope and longing.

STUDY GUIDE

SESSION 1 - *Chapters 1 & 2*

a. Have you, or anyone you know, experienced a 'break-in' (pp.8-11) of God's presence? Describe it.

b. With reference to pp.22-23, is your church growing in any of the four dimensions? If not why not?

SESSION 2 - *Chapter 3*

a. In what ways do you consider us to be living in a modern Babylon?

b. What signs of hope do you see today?

SESSION 3 - *Chapters 4 & 5*

a. Assess the strengths and weaknesses of 'inherited church' and 'emerging church'. What experience do you have of these?

b. Is worship feeding and inspiring your existing congregation? It not why not?

SESSION 4 - *Chapter 6*

a. With reference to pp.75-79, what would the writer of Ephesians be commending in your church?

b. What in your church would the writer be concerned about (pp.79-87)? What are you doing about it?

SESSION 5 - *Chapter 7*

a. 'The Church in Britain is living in a sort of Babylonian exile.' Comment

b. What should your church be relinquishing (p.96)? What should your church be seeking to receive?

SESSION 6 - *Chapter 8*

a. What do you agree/disagree with in chapter 8?

b. What will the future Methodist Church look like?

SESSION 7 - *Chapter 9*

a. Wesley says 'Know your disease! Know your cure! What should repentance mean for the Methodist Church as an organisation?

b.   What does repentance mean for your church? For you personally?

Read the Preface first and maybe the Appendix. This will give you some idea of what the book is about. Although seven sessions are indicated you may wish to collate sessions. I suggest members read the chapters indicated before you meet in your group to discuss.

The questions are for guidance only. It is important to deal with the issues and comments raised by your group and to talk and prayer about them.

There is now a follow-up to this book entitled
Methodism Unfinished.
Price £4.99

Obtainable from me
www.tomstuckey.me.uk

Books by Tom Stuckey

Understanding New Testament Letters Today	1985
Understanding Old Testament Prophets Today	1985
Rainbow, Journey and Feast: Biblical Covenants and a Theology of Mission	1988
Into the Far Country: A Theology of Mission for an Age of Violence	2003
Beyond the Box: Mission Challenges from John's Gospel	2005
On the Edge of Pentecost: A Theological Journey of Transformation	2007
The Wrath of God Satisfied? Atonement in an age of Violence	2012
Methodism Unfinished: Studies based on the reflections of ten Methodists	2019

Most of these can be obtained from Amazon, some in a Kindle version.

Printed in Poland
by Amazon Fulfillment
Poland Sp. z o.o., Wrocław